D0051024

For current pricing information,
or to learn more about this or any Nextext title,
call us toll-free at **1-800-323-5435**
or visit our web site at www.nextext.com.

A HISTORICAL READER

The VIETNAM War

Cover photograph: *U.S. soldiers on patrol in Vietnam, November 1965.*
Copyright © Co Rentmeester

Copyright © 2000 by McDougal Littell, a Houghton Mifflin Company.
All rights reserved. Nextext® is an imprint of McDougal Littell.

No part of this work may be reproduced or transmitted in any form or by
any means, electronic or mechanical, including photocopying and recording,
or by any information storage or retrieval system without prior written
permission of McDougal Littell unless such copying is expressly permitted by
federal copyright law. With the exception of not-for-profit transcription in
Braille, McDougal Littell is not authorized to grant permission for further
uses of copyrighted selections reprinted in this text without the permission
of their owners. Permission must be obtained from the individual copyright
owners identified herein. Address inquiries to Manager, Rights and
Permissions, McDougal Littell, P. O. Box 1667, Evanston, Illinois 60204.

Printed in the United States of America
ISBN 0-618-00369-X

2 3 4 5 6 7 — QKT — 06 05 04 03 02 01 00

Table of Contents

PART V: THE TET OFFENSIVE
AND THE AMERICAN WITHDRAWAL

Throughout the reader, vocabulary words appear in boldface
type and are footnoted. Specialized or technical words and phrases
appear in lightface type and are footnoted.

Introduction

Ambush

BY TIM O'BRIEN

When she was nine, my daughter Kathleen asked if I had ever killed anyone. She knew about the war; she knew I'd been a soldier. "You keep writing war stories," she said, "so I guess you must've killed somebody." It was a difficult moment, but I did what seemed right, which was to say, "Of course not," and then to take her onto my lap and hold her for a while. Someday, I hope, she'll ask again. But here I want to pretend she's a grown-up. I want to tell her exactly what happened, or what I remember happening, and then I want to say to her that as a little girl she was absolutely right. This is why I keep writing war stories:

He was a short, slender young man of about twenty. I was afraid of him—afraid of something—and as he passed me on the trail I threw a grenade that exploded at his feet and killed him.

Or to go back:

Shortly after midnight we moved into the **ambush**[1] site outside My Khe. The whole platoon was there, spread out in the dense brush along the trail, and for five hours nothing at all happened. We were working in two-man teams—one man on guard while the other slept, switching off every two hours—and I remember it was still dark when Kiowa shook me awake for the final watch. The night was foggy and hot. For the first few moments I felt lost, not sure about directions, groping for my helmet and weapon. I reached out and found three grenades and lined them up in front of me; the pins had already been straightened for quick throwing. And then for maybe half an hour I kneeled there and waited. Very gradually, in tiny slivers, dawn began to break through the fog, and from my position in the brush I could see ten or fifteen meters up the trail. The mosquitoes were fierce. I remember slapping them, wondering if I should wake up Kiowa and ask for some repellent, then thinking it was a bad idea, then looking up and seeing the young man come out of the fog. He wore black clothing and rubber sandals and a gray ammunition belt. His shoulders were slightly stooped, his head cocked to the side as if listening for something. He seemed at ease. He carried his weapon in one hand, muzzle down, moving without any hurry up the center of the trail. There was no sound at all—none that I can remember. In a way, it seemed, he was part of the morning fog, or my own imagination, but there was also the reality of what was happening in my stomach. I had already pulled the pin on a grenade. I had come up to a crouch. It was entirely automatic. I did not hate the young man; I did not see him as the enemy; I did not ponder issues of morality or politics or military duty. I crouched and kept my head low. I tried to swallow whatever was rising from my stomach, which tasted

---

[1] **ambush**—a sudden attack made from a concealed position.

like lemonade, something fruity and sour. I was terrified. There were no thoughts about killing. The grenade was to make him go away—just evaporate—and I leaned back and felt my mind go empty and then felt it fill up again. I had already thrown the grenade before telling myself to throw it. The brush was thick and I had to lob it high, not aiming, and I remember the grenade seeming to freeze above me for an instant, as if a camera had clicked, and I remember ducking down and holding my breath and seeing little wisps of fog rise from the earth. The grenade bounced once and rolled across the trail. I did not hear it, but there must've been a sound, because the young man dropped his weapon and began to run, just two or three quick steps, then he hesitated, swiveling to his right, and he glanced down at the grenade and tried to cover his head but never did. It occurred to me then that he was about to die. I wanted to warn him. The grenade made a popping noise—not soft but not loud either—not what I'd expected—and there was a puff of dust and smoke—a small white puff—and the young man seemed to jerk upward as if pulled by invisible wires. He fell on his back. His rubber sandals had been blown off. There was no wind. He lay at the center of the trail, his right leg bent beneath him, his one eye shut, his other eye a huge star-shaped hole.

It was not a matter of live or die. There was no real **peril**.[2] Almost certainly the young man would have passed by. And it will always be that way.

Later, I remember, Kiowa tried to tell me that the man would've died anyway. He told me that it was a good kill, that I was a soldier and this was a war, that I should shape up and stop staring and ask myself what the dead man would've done if things were reversed.

---

[2] **peril**—imminent danger.

None of it mattered. The words seemed far too complicated. All I could do was gape at the fact of the young man's body.

Even now I haven't finished sorting it out. Sometimes I forgive myself, other times I don't. In the ordinary hours of life I try not to dwell on it, but now and then, when I'm reading a newspaper or just sitting alone in a room, I'll look up and see the young man coming out of the morning fog. I'll watch him walk toward me, his shoulders slightly stooped, his head cocked to the side, and he'll pass within a few yards of me and suddenly smile at some secret thought and then continue up the trail to where it bends back into the fog.

QUESTIONS TO CONSIDER

1. Why does Tim O'Brien tell his daughter that he has never killed anyone?

2. How is the incident with the man in sandals "not a matter of live or die"?

3. What can you infer from O'Brien's daydream in the last paragraph?

A War Ends,
A War Begins

Settlement at Geneva

BY BERNARD B. FALL

In the seventeenth century, French traders and missionaries
arrived in southeast Asia. This eventually led to military domination
of the region, and in 1884 the French declared a **protectorate**[1]
over what is now Vietnam, known to the French as Indochina.
The Japanese occupied Vietnam during World War II, opposed by
Vietnamese nationalists. In 1946, the French returned and tried to
reassert their power, beginning a vicious war, which only ended in
1954 when the French were defeated at the Battle of Dien Bien
Phu. At the peace conference in Geneva, Switzerland, Vietnam was
divided into two parts: the South ruled by the Vietnamese emperor
Bao Dai and the North under the control of the Viet Minh, a
coalition of nationalist and Communist groups who had led the
fight against the French. The unification of the country was to occur
in 1956 after elections determined who would lead the country.

---

[1] **protectorate**—a relationship of protection and partial control assumed
by a superior power over a dependent country or region.

Soon after the cease-fire in Korea, in July, 1953, Communist equipment and advisers began to flow more plentifully to Ho Chi Minh's Viet-Minh forces fighting the French in Indochina. Pressure began to build up in France for a negotiated settlement along Korean lines. At the Bermuda conference of December, 1953, President Eisenhower, Prime Minister Churchill, and Premier Joseph Laniel of France decided to discuss the Indochina problem with the Soviet Union at the foreign-minister level.

The foreign ministers, meeting in Berlin, in February, 1954, agreed to a conference of interested powers to discuss both Korea and Indochina, to be held at Geneva toward the end of April, 1954. That was the signal for General Vo Nguyen Giap, Ho's Commander in Chief, to deliver a stunning blow to the French in Indochina, so as to strengthen his side's negotiating position to the utmost.

When the conference began at Geneva on April 27, the ghastly news of the agony of Dien Bien Phu completely overshadowed the Korean part of the negotiation, which soon **quagmired**[2] into a stalemate. By the time the delegates turned to Indochina on May 8, 1954, Dien Bien Phu had fallen a few hours earlier, and France's Foreign Minister, Georges Bidault, his voice choked with tears, could do little else but to begin the discussion with a eulogy to his country's fallen heroes.

But in areas other than Dien Bien Phu, the war was not going well for France, either. Indeed, only in South Viet-Nam proper was the situation at all encouraging. Terrorism in Saigon had been brought to an almost total standstill, and the Buddhist Cao-Dai and Hoa-Hao sects and Roman Catholic militia units had cleared extensive sections of the Mekong Delta of Viet-Minh control. But the determining factor was the deteriorating situation in the North: Vietnamese morale fell rapidly as the situation worsened.

---

[2] **quagmired**—got stuck in mud or muck.

The Vietnamese National Army, created by France in 1948, counted about 200,000 regulars and 50,000 village militiamen by February, 1954, while another 30,000 Vietnamese served within the 178,000-man French Expeditionary Force in Indochina and another 50,000 Cambodians and Laotians served in the armies of their own countries in the struggle against the Viet-Minh.

On the Communist side, Ho Chi Minh's forces had come a long way from the badly armed guerrilla bands of the mid-1940s. The Viet-Nam People's Army now comprised seven hard-core divisions abundantly equipped with modern American weapons captured by the Chinese in Korea and passed along. The Communist forces, with fewer than 100,000 regulars, 50,000 regional semiregulars, and about 225,000 local guerrillas, were numerically inferior to the French Union troops, but in a type of war where experts believe that the defending force must hold a 10-to-1 superiority in order to win (in 1965 the South Vietnamese and American forces hold a 5-to-1 lead over the Viet-Cong), the French 1.2-to-1 edge made the military contest—all other factors aside—well-nigh hopeless.

The French felt that the only way to tip the scales in their favor—or at least to prevent an outright military disaster—would be an open military commitment by the United States on their behalf. An American Military Assistance Advisory Group (MAAG) to the French forces in Indochina had been set up as early as July, 1950, and American financial and matériel aid to Indochina had totaled an actual expenditure of $1 billion by the time the fighting stopped.

But the United States was reluctant, so soon after the Korean War,[3] to become embroiled again in an Asian

---

[3] Korean War—In the Korean War (1950–1953), a U.S.-dominated United Nations coalition came to the aid of South Korea when North Korea, which was aided by the USSR and allied with Communist China, invaded. The war ended in a stalemate.

conflict—and one in support of a colonial power, at that. Britain was eager not to jeopardize the chances of a **détente**[4] between East and West over what seemed a marginal issue at best, and a lost cause at worst.

Besides the Western "big three," the other participants in the talks were the French-sponsored State of Viet-Nam, Laos, and Cambodia on the one hand and, on the other, the Viet-Minh's Democratic Republic of Viet-Nam, Russia, and Communist China. Britain and Russia, in the persons of Foreign Secretary Anthony Eden and Foreign Minister Vyacheslav Molotov, were co-chairmen.

At first, the Saigon delegation insisted on territorial unity for all of Viet-Nam and national elections under U.N. supervision. Considering the progress of the war, the Western powers felt that partition would be unavoidable. The Viet-Minh delegation, like Saigon, at first opted for nationwide elections, but after a hurried meeting between China's Premier Chou En-lai and Ho, it agreed to accept partition into "temporary regroupment areas."

What followed then was merely a "battle of the parallels," attempts by both sides to enlarge the zones allotted them and to fill in the details of the armistice supervisory machinery—all punctuated by further bad news for the French and Vietnamese as their military efforts failed and Saigon's administrative machinery slowly disintegrated.

The American delegation, under pressure from home not to give the impression of "approving" a "surrender to Communism," had for all practical purposes ceased to influence events. Secretary Dulles had left Geneva on May 4, even before the Indochina conference began. In President Eisenhower's words, the "American delegation [was] downgraded to an 'observer' mission." This attempt at saving face at home was to have important consequences as the negotiations reached their climax.

---

[4] **détente**—the easing of tensions between nations or political groups.

It must be remembered that the Geneva agreements were *military cease-fire* agreements, though negotiated at the highest political and diplomatic level. The actual signature of the agreements and their ultimate execution were to be reserved to *military* authorities on both sides.

On July 20, agreement was reached on Viet-Nam when the hitherto **intractable**[5] Molotov relented and made the Viet-Minh accept the 17th parallel as the cease-fire line (though it meant relinquishing territory they held in the south). Separate agreements on Laos and Cambodia remained to be worked out, but by about 2 o'clock the next morning the package was completed.

Brigadier General Henri Delteil, representing the French Army High Command in Indochina, signed first. Brigadier General Ta Quang Buu, Oxford-educated and a former leader of the French-sponsored Vietnamese Boy Scout Movement, signed for the Viet-Minh and invited Delteil to share a glass of champagne with him. Delteil quietly said: "I am sure that you understand that this is not possible." At 3:43 A.M. of July 21, 1954, the First Indochina War was over. . . .

In Viet-Nam itself, the state of affairs which resulted from the Geneva settlement was grim: 860,000 refugees—more than 500,000 of them Catholics—began to pour into what was now rapidly becoming "South Viet-Nam"—i.e., Viet-Nam south of the new demarcation line at the 17th parallel. North of the line, stolid-faced Viet-Minh regulars began to occupy the cities and towns left behind by withdrawing French troops.

Some 190,000 Franco-Vietnamese troops moved south of the demarcation line, although many of the Vietnamese whose home villages were in the North preferred to desert in order not to be separated from their families. In the South, it is now admitted (though it was carefully hushed up at the time), perhaps as many as

---

[5] **intractable**—difficult to manage or govern; stubborn.

80,000 local guerrillas and regulars and their dependents, including almost 10,000 mountain tribesmen,
went northward.

Perhaps another 5,000 to 6,000 local hard-core guerrillas—probably the elite of the Viet-Minh's military and
political operators in the South—simply went underground. They hid their weapons and radio equipment
and became anonymous villagers—at least for a while.
In the cities, others, such as the Viet-Cong's present
leader, Nguyen Huu Tho, created "legal struggle"
with the aim of **propagating**[6] the new catch-phrase of
"peace and reunification in two years." They, however,
were soon disbanded or arrested by the Saigon police.

In Saigon, the fledgling Diem regime was trying to
cope both with the administrative chaos resulting from
partition and the influx of refugees, and with the chal-
lenges against its survival from various political and
religious groups and sects. The government's chances of
surviving even as long as the two-year election deadline
were rated as poor. President Eisenhower summed up
the situation in his memoirs:

> I have never talked or corresponded with a per-
> son knowledgeable in Indochinese affairs who
> did not agree that had elections been held as of
> the time of the fighting, possibly 80 per cent of
> the population would have voted for the
> Communist Ho Chi Minh as their leader rather
> than Chief of State Bao-Dai.

Since the North controlled a population of more
than 15 million and the South fewer than 12 million,
and since the North could be trusted to "deliver" its
electorate in overwhelming numbers, such an election
would beyond a doubt have resulted in a peaceful

---

[6] **propagating**—spreading.

takeover of all of Viet-Nam by Ho Chi Minh in July, 1956. (It is worth noting that Diem disposed of Bao-Dai by a rigged **plebiscite,**[7] held in 1955. Diem got 98.8 per cent of the vote. Diem was overthrown and assassinated in a coup in 1963; Bao-Dai is now[8] living in France.)

Little wonder, then, that the Diem government almost immediately took the position that the Geneva agreements, signed by a foreign military command (i.e., the French) "in contempt of Vietnamese national interests," were not binding upon it. It not only refused to consult with its northern counterpart about elections, but it also turned down repeated proposals by North Viet-Nam to normalize economic and postal regulations, arguing that "we cannot entertain any Communist proposal as long as we do not have evidence that they place the interests of the Fatherland above those of Communism."

That attitude amounted in fact to an economic blockade—which hurt, for North Viet-Nam had until then received an average of more than 200,000 tons a year of southern rice to cover its internal food deficit.

The French, already embroiled in the beginnings of a new colonial war in Algeria,[9] offered little argument when the Diem regime requested in February, 1956 (that is, before the July deadline on elections), that they withdraw their troops. The French High Command in Indochina, which had been the formal signer of the 1954 Geneva agreements, was dissolved on April 26, 1956. Some hotheads in Saigon toyed with the idea of declaring the Geneva accords **null.**[10] Indeed, carefully coached mobs ransacked the Saigon offices and billets of the International Commission for

---

[7] **plebiscite**—a vote by which the people of an entire country express an opinion on a choice of government or ruler.

[8] This article was written in May, 1965.

[9] new colonial war in Algeria—In the Algerian War (1954–1962), Muslim Algerians fought for and won their country's independence from France.

[10] **null**—invalid.

Supervision and Control on the first anniversary of the Geneva cease-fire.

But cooler counsel prevailed (some say, at American behest) and a few days before the July, 1956, deadline for national elections, the South Vietnamese Foreign Secretary, while denouncing the validity of the agreements, established what he called "*de facto* cooperation" with the ICSC. The joint Commissions, however, were soon abolished; Saigon argued that the North Vietnamese members stationed in Saigon were engaging in subversive activities and obtained their recall in 1957.

QUESTIONS TO CONSIDER

1. Who are the Viet Minh?

2. What is the Indochina "problem"?

3. Why is the U.S. reluctant to come to the aid of the French in Vietnam?

Diem Defeats His Own Best Troops

BY STANLEY KARNOW

The government established in South Vietnam by the terms of the Geneva Accords (see pages 16–23) was lead by Ngo Dinh Diem, a French- and American-educated nationalist. Diem was supported by the United States because he was anti-Communist, yet Diem had no political following in Vietnam itself. The North was led by the Communist Ho Chi Minh, and the U.S. feared that if the country were unified by elections, the Communists would come to power. In 1956, with U.S. backing, Diem refused to hold the planned referendum, beginning Vietnam's third war of independence. The U.S. offered vast amounts of arms and money to "save" South Vietnam. Yet it was difficult to save Diem's government because it had no popular following. The Viet Minh, who held power in North Vietnam, had little trouble recruiting guerrillas to fight Diem in the South. By the middle of 1957, a war was underway in the South. Diem's unpopularity is described below in a report on one of the coups attempted against Diem and his rule.

SAIGON—At three one humid morning last November, three battalions of paratroopers surrounded the handsome Saigon palace of South Vietnam's President Ngo Dinh Diem. Within thirty-six hours, their attempted revolt had been crushed. The rebel chiefs fled to sanctuary in Cambodia, and the rebel troops themselves, forced to surrender, tactfully reaffirmed their allegiance to the régime. Bullet holes in buildings were quickly plastered in. The dead were discreetly buried. President Diem, who has survived several serious scrapes in his six years of power, emerged from the fortified cellar of his palace with another narrow triumph to his credit. "The government continues to serve the nation," he intoned confidently, and his spokesmen dismissed the abortive *coup d'état* as merely "an incident."

So it was—just an incident. But it was the most dramatic symptom to date of a deeper disturbance that has plagued South Vietnam for a year or more. Beneath the appearance of calm and stability, and despite all the government's assurances of security, President Diem's régime may well be approaching collapse, and with such a collapse, the country could fall to the Communists. "The situation is desperate," an official told me a few weeks ago.

Bands of Communist guerrillas, directed from Hanoi in North Vietnam, roam almost every rural region, blowing up bridges, blocking roads, terrorizing farmers, and attacking army posts. This menace has been compounded by the demoralization of the peasants, the army, and what the French-oriented Vietnamese call *"les intellectuels."* Most serious of all, perhaps, is President Diem's own attitude. He seems to have survived the revolt with his ego unscathed and his faith in his own infallibility renewed.

Diem is a complex personality. From his mixed Catholic and Confucian[1] background evolved a combination of monk and mandarin,[2] a kind of **ascetic**[3] authoritarian. He is a deceptively dainty-looking man; in fact, he is tough and obstinate. To a significant degree, his stubborn self-righteousness saved a régime that most "experts" considered lost back in 1955, after the Geneva Agreement had divided South Vietnam at the seventeenth parallel. Amply bolstered by American sympathy and material aid—which has totaled more than a billion dollars in the past five years—he successfully fought off the **insurgent**[4] sects, consolidated a government, welcomed and resettled almost a million refugees from the Communist North. He initiated a land-reform program and embarked upon such ambitious projects as building roads and railways, extending agricultural credit, and establishing light industries.

In all his energetic enterprises, the fixation in Diem's mind has been survival. But in his concentration on survival, Diem seems to have paralyzed rather than inspired those around him. He demands absolute loyalty and has developed an inability or unwillingness to trust others. Instead, fearful of betrayal, impatient with any initiative by underlings, he has gathered all power to himself, and working as much as fifteen hours a day, he plunges into the most minute details of administration, personally signing passport applications, reserving for himself the right to approve a student's scholarship to the United States. He has even been known to decide on the distance between roadside trees.

This sort of one-man rule is not uncommon in underdeveloped countries that lack trained personnel.

---

[1] Confucian—of or having to do with Confucius (551–479 B.C.), a Chinese philosopher and moral teacher.

[2] mandarin—a high government official or bureaucrat.

[3] **ascetic**—leading a life of self-discipline and self-denial, especially for spiritual improvement.

[4] **insurgent**—rebellious.

But it discourages the development of a responsible civil service, and it can inspire minor officials to all sorts of red tape and pettifoggery.[5] Without any balanced administrative structure, officials turn to the most convenient source of power. Here, Diem's family—he does trust them—display their peculiar talents. They have succeeded in building a partly public, partly **clandestine**[6] structure inside and outside the government. On this, Diem's power rests.

One of the President's brothers, the mysterious Ngo Dinh Can, lives in Hué, and from there controls central Vietnam. He exercises much of his authority through the National Revolutionary Movement, the pro-government political party. Another brother, Ngo Dinh Nhu, whom Diem trusts implicitly and relies upon constantly, is probably the most powerful single individual in the country after Diem himself. Educated in Paris and the leading native civil servant under French rule, Nhu is a handsome, articulate, passionate, voluble intellectual. Speaking elegant French in a voice that sometimes whines with emotion, he will declaim at length on one of his favorite subjects, the "problems of the underdeveloped country." This includes an exposition of the theory that "freedom must not prevent the march of progress."

There is considerable validity to Nhu's notion. But his ideas in action are somewhat more questionable. He has certainly helped to curtail freedom, but it is not so sure that he has done much to promote progress. He directs an **avowedly**[7] clandestine movement called the Can Lao Nhan Vi—the "Revolutionary Labor Party"— which, he concedes frankly, is organized along the lines of a Communist apparatus. Its seventy thousand secret members have been infiltrated into factories, villages,

---

[5] pettifoggery—trickery.

[6] **clandestine**—kept or done in secret, often in order to conceal an illicit or improper purpose.

[7] **avowedly**—openly.

government offices, army units, schools, and newspapers, where they spend part of their time collecting information about their compatriots. Nhu's pretty wife—commonly called Madame Nhu, though the family surname is Ngo—commands the ladies' auxiliary.

Although there is not a single shred of evidence against them, Nhu and his wife are believed to be at the heart of most major corruption in the country. Through his Can Lao, Nhu is said to control the wood and charcoal trade, and there are tales of his investments in Brazil, France, and Switzerland. When the Nhus are confronted with stories of their supposed **venality,**[8] they simply issue denials. "It's the diplomats," Madame Nhu told me huffily during a recent chat. "They have nothing better to do than gossip. I just ignore them." Her husband tends to protest more vigorously. "Foreign powers are against us," he insists. "Everyone picks on poor little Ngo Dinh Diem and his brothers. Why? Maybe it's because we are Catholic. I don't know. But these rumors of our corruption, our stealing—all lies. Nobody has any proof."

One way or the other, however, everyone believes that the Nhus are corrupt (everyone, that is, but Diem himself, who will not even listen to charges against his family). The real or imaginary, or total or partial, misconduct of Diem's family is serious because it coincides with a period of tension generated by increased Communist terrorism. And as Communist terrorism became more acute, the growing uneasiness and insecurity sparked more vocal dissatisfaction which, not long ago, began to spread beyond the family to criticism of Diem himself. . . .

In all the recent Saigon grumbling, however, there has been surprisingly little demand for "democracy." The general displeasure, as I heard it, was with what the

---

[8] **venality**—susceptibility to bribery or corruption, as in the use of a position of trust for dishonest gain.

wits dubbed "Diemocracy"—the government's make-believe guarantees of civil liberties and fair elections. With much fanfare, extensive plans were worked out for National Assembly elections in August, 1959, and opponents of the government's National Revolutionary Movement were invited to run. But hardly had the campaign begun than opposition politicians encountered a variety of obstacles, such as having the wrong stamp or signature on their documents or displaying "illegal" placards. Those who managed to hurdle these barriers found themselves facing another block on election day. Contingents of troops were moved into Saigon, where the opposition was strongest; the troops were all under orders to vote for the government candidates.

Even so, a Harvard-educated opponent of the régime, Dr. Phan Quang Dan, somehow succeeded in winning a parliament seat. He was never able to assume it, however. With almost infantile **pique**,[9] the government arrested him for such infractions as opening his campaign "too early," using "unauthorized posters," and making "false promises"; and despite appeals by three western ambassadors to Diem, Dr. Dan's election was annulled.

Although nobody was prepared to fight strongly for Dr. Dan, the government's action against him made Diem appear petty and peevish, and it diminished his prestige considerably. Last April, a group of eighteen former officials—among them several ex-ministers, the president of the Red Cross and, in spite of family ties, Madame Nhu's uncle—sent Diem a petition requesting that he "liberalize his régime, expand democracy, grant minimum civil rights," and reform the administration, the army, and the economy. Neither this modest appeal nor its signers could have been considered a menace to the régime.

---

[9] **pique**—wounded pride; childish resentment.

Upon receipt of their petition, however, President Diem's first reaction was to have them arrested and sent to "political re-education camps," where an estimated 25,000 citizens are currently being shown the paths of righteousness. After some reflection, Diem decided to ignore them. But, coincidentally, about thirty obscure doctors, students, and journalists were picked up on suspicion of "Communist affiliations." To my knowledge, none of them—nor any other suspects—has ever been brought to trial. Frequent police roundups of this kind serve as a warning. . . .

In that sort of atmosphere it is usually difficult to assess public opinion. But in Saigon that week I discovered, on the contrary, a greater willingness in people to talk than I had ever before encountered. They had, it seems on looking back, a desire to unburden themselves **engendered**[10] by a mixture of confused feelings: desperation at the rebel failure, encouragement from the attempt, and, I found everywhere, the certainty that sooner or later there would be another revolt—a successful one. "The army has lost its virginity," as a knowledgeable Vietnamese put it. "Next time it will be easier."

South Vietnam will be fortunate, however, if the "next time" there is fighting in Saigon, the antigovernment forces are not Communists. For the revolt and its aftermath is bound to prove a boon to the guerrillas. It introduced an element of distrust between Diem and his army that should inevitably make their relations more brittle than ever. Beyond that, the insurrection took a moral and physical toll on the most effective army unit in the country. The paratroopers were the spearhead against the Communist partisans. From their bases around Saigon, they could be mobilized and put into action anywhere within eighteen hours. Although

---

[10] **engendered**—brought into existence.

no casualty figures have been released, it is calculated that as many as four hundred of them may have been killed during the revolt. Some of their best officers fled with the rebel colonels; and nobody knows how many individual soldiers, beaten and ashamed, deserted to the jungles. A high-ranking apolitical military man commented sadly: "The Communists would have given three divisions to wipe out the paratroopers. We have done it for them."

If the insurrection hurt the army, it also shattered Diem's prestige. The aloof mandarin had never been loved, but he had at least enjoyed a healthy measure of respect. Diem lost ground by allowing the situation to degenerate to a point at which revolt was conceivable, especially by troops who had often served as his most trusted bodyguard. Moreover, he lost face badly by **disavowing**[11] the promises of reform he had broadcast during the uprising. "We didn't want the rebels to harm him," a schoolteacher said bitterly, "but now we're sorry they didn't."

---

[11] **disavowing**—disclaiming knowledge of, responsibility for, or association with.

QUESTIONS TO CONSIDER

1. In what way was the November revolt a "symptom of a deeper disturbance" in South Vietnam?

2. How would you describe the major criticisms of Ngo Dinh Diem's government?

3. What was the mood in Saigon during 1957?

A "Very Real War" in Vietnam— and the Deep U.S. Commitment

BY HOMER BIGART

U.S. support for South Vietnam and Diem had begun under President Dwight D. Eisenhower, and it continued under John F. Kennedy, who felt that the U.S. must expand its presence there to take the decisive steps to beat the Communists. In November, 1961, Kennedy began sending U.S. soldiers as military advisors to the South Vietnamese: 3,205 in 1962, rising to 16,300 in 1963. This commitment of troops began the long U.S. involvement in Vietnam. In the following selection, from February 1962, the famed New York Times *war correspondent Homer Bigart describes the advisors' role in Vietnam.*

SAIGON, Feb. 24—The United States is involved in a war in Vietnam. American troops will stay until victory.

That is what Attorney General Robert Kennedy said here last week. He called it "war . . . in a very real sense of the word." He said that President Kennedy had pledged that the United States would stand by South Vietnam's President Ngo Dinh Diem "until we win."

At the moment the war isn't going badly for "our" side. There is a lull in Viet Cong activities, and the South Vietnamese forces are both expanding and shaping up better as a fighting force. But all that is needed to **precipitate**[1] a major war is for the Chinese Communists and Communist North Vietnam to react to a build-up of American forces.

American support to Vietnam has always been based on the fear that Communist control of this country would jeopardize all Southeast Asia. And it continues despite the fact that Diem's American critics—especially liberals repelled by the dictatorial aspects of his regime—have been predicting his imminent downfall.

Diem remains firmly in charge and Washington's support for his regime today seems more passionate and inflexible than ever.

Actually the United States has been deeply involved in the fate of Vietnam since 1949 when the decision was made to subsidize the continuation of French rule against the Viet Minh rebellion. The first United States Military Assistance Advisory Group (M.A.A.G.) arrived in 1951 to supervise the distribution of supplies.

Thereafter the United States played an increasingly important role. To use a favorite Washington term, aid

---

[1] **precipitate**—cause to happen, especially suddenly or prematurely.

was "escalated" until today $2 billion has been sunk into Vietnam with no end to the outlay in sight.

This may sound more reckless than the best brinkmanship[2] of John Foster Dulles' days, and perhaps it is. But the United States is on this particular faraway brink because the Kennedy Administration seems convinced that the Communists won't rise to the challenge of the American presence and assistance.

The battle in Vietnam currently involves some 300,000 armed South Vietnamese and 3,000 American servicemen on one side, against 18,000 to 25,000 Viet Cong Communist regulars operating as guerrillas.

The battle that is being fought is complex—in the nature of the fighting, in the internal political background and in its international implications.

The United States does not have any combat infantry troops in Vietnam as of now, but we are getting ready for that possibility. Marine Corps officers have completed ground **reconnaissance**[3] in the central Vietnam highlands, a potential theater of large-scale action between American troops and Communist forces coming down from the north.

American combat troops are not likely to be thrown into Vietnam unless Communist North Vietnam moves across the seventeenth parallel or pushes large forces down through Laos into South Vietnam,

In that case the United States would have to move in fast. Forty miles below the frontier with North Vietnam and parallel to it is Highway 9. This road has high strategic importance. Not only is it one of the few adequate roads open across the mountains to the

---

[2] brinkmanship—the practice, especially in international politics, of seeking advantage by creating the impression that one is willing and able to push a highly dangerous situation to the limit rather than concede.

[3] **reconnaissance**—an inspection or exploration of an area, especially one made to gather military information.

Laotian border but it extends across Laos to Savannakhet on the Mekong River frontier with Thailand. If Highway 9 could be held from the Mekong to the sea by American, Vietnamese, Laotian and Thai forces, South Vietnam might be saved.

The situation right now is far more stable than it was last September, when the Communists were attacking in battalion strength and were even able to seize and hold a provincial capital, Phuoc Vinh, for a few hours. The September action seemed a prelude to an all-out Communist drive to overturn the Diem Government. It precipitated the present flood of American military advisors and service troops.

Today American warships are helping the **embryonic**[4] Vietnamese Navy to guard the sea frontier against infiltration from North Vietnam and U.S. Navy servicemen presently will arrive to help clean out guerrillas from the maze of tidal waterways in the Mekong River delta. The U.S. Army helicopter crews have come under fire taking Vietnamese combat troops into guerrilla zones or carrying pigs and other livestock to hungry outposts surrounded by hostile country. U.S. Air Force pilots have flown with Vietnamese pilots on bombing missions against reported enemy concentrations and against two frontier forts recently evacuated by the Vietnamese Army.

So far our contribution in blood has been small. One American sergeant has been killed by enemy action and another is missing and presumed captured. Inevitably our casualties will grow. . . .

The man who is at the center of the Vietnamese effort and who is also a center of controversy—President Diem—is something of an **enigma**.[5] He is a mandarin (an aristocrat) and a devout Catholic. So there are two strikes against him at the start, for mandarins were

---

[4] **embryonic**—in an early stage of development.

[5] **enigma**—one that is puzzling, ambiguous, or inexplicable.

regarded by the masses as greedy and corrupt, and Catholics as an unpopular minority.

Diem, however, has proved incorruptible. Rumors of personal enrichment of members of his family have never been proved. And Diem has been careful not to arouse Buddhist hostility. He is a man of great personal courage, but he is suspicious and mistrustful. The creation of a central intelligence agency here was delayed for months until Diem found a director he could trust.

Diem, a 66-year-old bachelor, often has been accused of withdrawing inside his narrow family clique and divorcing himself from reality. Critics say he distrusts everyone except the family and takes advice only from his brothers, particularly Ngo Dinh Nhu, his political advisor. . . .

One former Diem adviser said he was shocked by the loss of support among the people in the past two years. He blamed this on the fact that Government seemed to grope from crisis to crisis without a clear policy: "It's just anti-Communist and not pro anything."

But another qualified observer, perhaps less biased, cautioned against underrating Diem. Increased guerrilla activity had not been matched, he said, by a corresponding rise in popular discontent and this failure to respond must have depressed the Communists.

Most villages, he added, were like a leaf in the wind: "When the Viet Cong enters, the population turns pro-Communist; when the Government troops arrive, sentiment shifts to the Government." But generally the village people would settle for the Government side, he said, not because they admired the Government but because they wanted peace.

Consequently the Government has a great advantage. He estimated that of the 30 percent tending to the Viet Cong, only a third were hard-core, another third would adhere to the Communists under adversity, while the remaining third would break off under pressure.

Freedom from dictatorship and freedom from foreign domination are major propaganda lines for the Viet Cong. Americans in uniform have now been seen by the peasants in virtually all sections of the country. This has given the Communists a chance to raise the bogey of foreign military domination.

The lack of trained troops to keep the Viet Cong under relentless pressure probably will continue to handicap the military command throughout 1962, because at least a year must elapse before the self-defense units will be really capable of defending their villages.

Whether because the Army is beginning to take the initiative and is penetrating secret areas of Viet Cong concentrations or because the Viet Cong has abated its activities in order to recruit and train, the fact remains that security seems better in most parts of Vietnam.

In peaceful, booming Saigon there is much speculation on how the Viet Cong will react to an American build-up. Senior American officers have been studying an enemy guide book to guerrilla warfare searching avidly for clues, as though this modest work were the Viet Cong's "Mein Kampf."[6]

There will never be enough troops to seal off the frontiers.

There aren't even enough troops to ring Viet Cong enclaves near Saigon. Not before summer, when the civil guard and self-defense units are slated to take over the burden of defending their villages will enough troops be freed for a counter-guerrilla offensive. Then, instead of a conventional setpiece offensive of limited duration, a counter-guerrilla drive will seek to keep Viet Cong units on the run at all times, tire them out by constant

---

[6] "Mein Kampf"—title of book published by Adolf Hitler that explained his facist philosophy.

pressure and force them into less hospitable country where food supplies are scarce.

The offensive cannot succeed unless the Government is able to mobilize positive popular support. This will be difficult, for the Government is just beginning to develop grass roots political cadres.

Meanwhile something more than narrowly anti-Communist goals must be offered Saigon intellectuals, who are now scorned by both Diem and the Americans. This group may be permanently alienated unless there is promise of democratic reforms. Without pressure from Washington, there is not likely to be any relaxation of Diem's personal dictatorship. The struggle will go on at least ten years, in the opinion of some observers, and severely test American patience.

The United States seems **inextricably**[7] committed to a long, inconclusive war. The Communists can prolong it for years. Even without large-scale intervention from the north, which would lead to "another Korea," what may be achieved at best is only restoration of a tolerable security similar to that achieved in Malaya after years of fighting. But it is too late to disengage; our prestige has been committed. Washington says we will stay until the finish.

---

[7] **inextricably**—unavoidably; inescapably.

QUESTIONS TO CONSIDER

1. In what ways did U.S. involvement in Vietnam change between 1949 and 1962, the year in which this article was written?

2. What does it mean to be "anti-Communist and not pro anything"?

3. Why does the U.S. government decide to go to war in Vietnam?

The Tonkin Gulf Incident

FROM *THE PENTAGON PAPERS*

With the assassination of President Kennedy in 1963, Lyndon Johnson became President of the United States, and he too was an ardent supporter of American intervention in Vietnam. Johnson wanted to expand American involvement and used two incidents in the Gulf of Tonkin in early August, 1964, to do this. On August 2, the American destroyer Maddox was attacked by North Vietnamese torpedo boats. Two days later, the Maddox's radar system again registered a torpedo attack. Because no ships were sighted and the destroyer was undamaged, it is now thought that the radar malfunctioned. Johnson asked Congress for a resolution that would allow him to "take all necessary measures" to prosecute the war. The Gulf of Tonkin Resolution was passed on August 7, which gave the president broad and unchecked powers to wage a war in Vietnam. In 1971, a secret Pentagon study of U.S. involvement in Vietnam, known as The Pentagon Papers, *came to light. In these papers was a detailed analysis of what had occurred in the Gulf of Tonkin incident.*

What happened in the Gulf? As noted earlier, U.S.S. MADDOX commenced the second DE SOTO Patrol on 31 July. On the prior night South Vietnamese coastal patrol forces made a midnight attack, including an **amphibious**[1] "commando" raid, on Hon Me and Hon Nieu Islands, about 19° N. latitude. At the time of this attack, U.S.S. MADDOX was 120–130 miles away just heading into waters off North Vietnam. On 2 August, having reached the northernmost point on its patrol track and having headed South, the destroyer was intercepted by three North Vietnamese patrol boats. Apparently, these boats and a fleet of **junks**[2] had moved into the area near the island to search for the attacking force and had mistaken *Maddox* for a South Vietnamese escort vessel. (Approximately eleven hours earlier, while on a northerly heading, *Maddox* had altered course to avoid the junk concentration shown on her radar; about six hours after that—now headed South—*Maddox* had altered her course to the southeast to avoid the junks a second time.) When the PT boats began their high-speed run at her, at a distance of approximately 10 miles, the destroyer was 28 miles from the coast and heading farther into international waters. Two of the boats closed to within 5,000 yards, launching one torpedo each. As they approached, *Maddox* fired on the boats with her 5-inch batteries and altered course to avoid the torpedoes, which were observed passing the starboard side at a distance of 100 to 200 yards. The third boat moved up abeam of the destroyer and took a direct 5-inch hit; it managed to launch a torpedo which failed to run. All three PT boats fired 50-caliber machine guns at *Maddox* as they made their firing runs, and a bullet fragment was recovered from the destroyer's

---

[1] **amphibious**—able to operate both on land and in water.

[2] **junks**—ships.

superstructure. The attacks occurred in mid-afternoon, and photographs were taken of the torpedo boats as they attacked.

Upon first report of the PT boats' apparently hostile intent, four F-8E aircraft were launched from the aircraft carrier *Ticonderoga*, many miles to the south, with instructions to provide air cover but not to fire unless they or *Maddox* were fired upon. As *Maddox* continued in a southerly direction, *Ticonderoga's* aircraft attacked the two boats that had initiated the action. Both were damaged with Zuni rockets and 20mm gunfire. . . .

QUESTIONS TO CONSIDER

1. What action did the North Vietnamese patrol boats take on August 2 and why?

2. Why do you think this incident led to the escalation of U.S. military effort in Vietnam?

Speeches

BY PRESIDENT LYNDON JOHNSON AND HO CHI MINH

With the power of the Gulf of Tonkin Resolution (see page 39), President Johnson began rapidly increasing American involvement in Vietnam. At the end of 1964 there were 23,300 U.S. soldiers in Vietnam; in twelve months that total rose to 184,300. And, in February 1965, the U.S. began bombing North Vietnam. In April 1965, Johnson gave a speech describing U.S. aims in Vietnam and why the U.S. needed to commit additional troops, munitions, and money. Ho Chi Minh, the leader of North Vietnam and the spiritual leader of the guerrilla movement in the South, gave a speech shortly after the one given by Johnson responding to the American president. Ho spoke to the Vietnamese people's own goals in the war.

Speech on April 7, 1965
by President Lyndon Johnson

Tonight Americans and Asians are dying for a world where each people may choose its own path to change.

This is the principle for which our ancestors fought in the valleys of Pennsylvania. It is the principle for which our sons fight tonight in the jungles of Viet-Nam.

Viet-Nam is far away from this quiet campus. We have no territory there, nor do we seek any. The war is dirty and brutal and difficult. And some 400 young men, born into an America that is bursting with opportunity and promise, have ended their lives on Viet-Nam's steaming soil.

Why must we take this painful road?

Why must this Nation hazard its case, and its interest, and its power for the sake of a people so far away?

We fight because we must fight if we are to live in a world where every country can shape its own destiny. And only in such a world will our own freedom be finally secure.

This kind of world will never be built by bombs or bullets. Yet the infirmities of man are such that force must often precede reason, and the waste of war, the works of peace.

We wish that this were not so. But we must deal with the world as it is, if it is ever to be as we wish.

THE NATURE OF THE CONFLICT

The world as it is in Asia is not a serene or peaceful place.

The first reality is that North Viet-Nam has attacked the independent nation of South Viet-Nam. Its object is total conquest.

Of course, some of the people of South Viet-Nam are participating in attack on their own government. But trained men and supplies, orders and arms, flow in a constant stream from north to south.

This support is the heartbeat of the war.

And it is a war of unparalleled brutality. Simple farmers are the targets of assassination and kidnapping. Women and children are strangled in the night because their men are loyal to their government. And helpless villages are ravaged by sneak attacks. Large-scale raids are conducted on towns, and terror strikes in the heart of cities.

The confused nature of this conflict cannot mask the fact that it is the new face of an old enemy.

Over this war—and all Asia—is another reality: the deepening shadow of Communist China. The rulers in Hanoi are urged on by Peking.[1] This is a regime which has destroyed freedom in Tibet, which has attacked India, and has been condemned by the United Nations for aggression in Korea. It is a nation which is helping the forces of violence in almost every continent. The contest in Viet-Nam is part of a wider pattern of aggressive purposes.

Why are these realities our concern? Why are we in South Viet-Nam?

We are there because we have a promise to keep. Since 1954 every American President has offered support to the people of South Viet-Nam. We have helped to build, and we have helped to defend. Thus, over many years, we have made a national pledge to help South Viet-Nam defend its independence.

And I intend to keep that promise.

To dishonor that pledge, to abandon this small and brave nation to its enemies, and to the terror that must follow, would be an unforgivable wrong.

We are also there to strengthen world order. Around the globe, from Berlin to Thailand, are people whose well-being rests, in part, on the belief that they can count on us if they are attacked. To leave Viet-Nam to its fate would shake the confidence of all these people in the value of an American commitment and in the value of America's word. The result would be increased unrest and instability, and even wider war.

We are also there because there are great stakes in the balance. Let no one think for a moment that retreat from Viet-Nam would bring an end to conflict. The battle

[1] Peking—an allusion to Communist Party leaders.

would be renewed in one country and then another. The central lesson of our time is that the appetite of aggression is never satisfied. To withdraw from one battlefield means only to prepare for the next. We must say in southeast Asia—as we did in Europe—in the words of the Bible: "Hitherto shalt thou come, but no further."

There are those who say that all our effort there will be futile—that China's power is such that it is bound to dominate all southeast Asia. But there is no end to that argument until all of the nations of Asia are swallowed up.

There are those who wonder why we have a responsibility there. Well, we have it there for the same reason that we have a responsibility for the defense of Europe. World War II was fought in both Europe and Asia, and when it ended we found ourselves with continued responsibility for the defense of freedom.

OUR OBJECTIVE IN VIET-NAM

Our objective is the independence of South Viet-Nam, and its freedom from attack. We want nothing for ourselves—only that the people of South Viet-Nam be allowed to guide their own country in their own way.

We will do everything necessary to reach that objective. And we will do only what is absolutely necessary. . . .

Speech to National Assembly on April 15, 1965
by Ho Chi Minh

Over the past ten years, the U.S. imperialists and their henchmen have carried out an extremely ruthless war and have caused much grief to our **compatriots**[2] in South Vietnam. Over the past few months, they have frenziedly expanded the war to North Vietnam.

---

[2] **compatriots**—people born or living in their own country.

In defiance of the 1954 Geneva Agreements and international law, they have sent hundreds of aircraft and dozens of warships to bomb and **strafe**[3] North Vietnam repeatedly. Laying bare themselves their piratical face, the U.S. aggressors are blatantly encroaching upon our country. They hope that by resorting to the force of weapons they can compel our 30 million compatriots to become their slaves. But they are grossly mistaken. They will certainly meet with **ignominious**[4] defeat.

Our Vietnamese people are a heroic people. Over the past ten years or more, our 14 million compatriots in the South have overcome all hardships, made every sacrifice and struggled very valiantly. Starting with their bare hands, they have seized guns from the enemy to fight against the enemy, have recorded victory after victory, and are launching a continual attack inflicting upon the U.S. aggressors and the traitors ever greater defeats and causing them to be bogged down more and more deeply. The greater their defeats, the more frantically they resort to the most cruel means, such as using napalm[5] bombs and toxic gas to massacre our compatriots in the South. It is because they are bogged down in South Vietnam they have furiously attacked North Vietnam.

. . . The U.S. imperialists are precisely the saboteurs of the Geneva Agreements, yet they have brazenly declared that because they wished to "restore peace" and "defend the Geneva Agreements" they brought U.S. troops to our country to carry out massacres and destruction. . . .

U.S. President Johnson has . . . loudly threatened to resort to violence to subdue our people. This is a

---

[3] **strafe**—attack (ground troops, for example) with a machine gun or cannon from a low-flying aircraft.

[4] **ignominious**—shameful; disgraceful.

[5] napalm—an explosively flammable mixture of polystyrene, benzene, and gasoline.

mere foolish illusion. Our people will definitely never be **subjugated.**[6] . . .

We love peace but we are not afraid of war. We are resolved to drive away the U.S. aggressors and to defend the freedom, independence, and territorial integrity of our Fatherland.

The people throughout our country are firmly confident that with their militant solidarity, valiant spirit, and creative wisdom, and with the sympathy and support of the world's peoples, they will certainly lead this great Resistance War to complete victory.

Our people are very grateful to and highly value the fraternal solidarity and assistance of the socialist countries, especially the Soviet Union and China, of the people in all continents who are actively supporting us in our struggle against the U.S. imperialist aggressors, the most cruel enemy of mankind. . . .

The American people have been duped by the propaganda of their government, which has extorted from them billions of dollars to throw into the crater of war. Thousands of American youths—their sons and brothers—have met a tragic death or have been pitifully wounded on the Vietnamese battlefields thousands of miles from the United States. At present, many mass organizations of individuals in the United States are demanding that their government at once stop this unjust war and withdraw U.S. troops from South Vietnam. Our people are resolved to drive away the U.S. imperialists, our sworn enemy. But we always express our friendship with the progressive American people. . . .

Our people are living in an extremely glorious period of history. Our country has the great honor of being an outpost of the socialist camp and of the world's

---

[6] **subjugated**—enslaved; made subservient.

peoples who are struggling against **imperialism,**[7] **colonialism,**[8] and **neocolonialism.**[9]

Our people have fought and made sacrifices not only for the sake of their own freedom and independence, but also for the common freedom and independence of the other peoples and for the peace in the world.

On the battlefront against the U.S. aggressors, our people's task is very heavy but also very glorious. . . .

I call on our compatriots and fighters to constantly heighten their revolutionary heroism, vigilance, and fighting spirit—to promote the "everyone redoubles his efforts" emulation movement, resolutely overcome all difficulties, endeavor to build and defend socialist North Vietnam and wholeheartedly support the patriotic struggle of our compatriots in the South!

Let all of us single-mindedly unite as one man and be determined to defeat the U.S. aggressors!

For the future of our Fatherland, for the happiness of our people, let all compatriots and fighters throughout the country valiantly march forward!

---

[7] **imperialism**—the policy of extending the rule of one country over other countries or colonies.

[8] **colonialism**—a policy by which a nation maintains or extends its control over foreign dependencies.

[9] **neocolonialism**—a policy whereby a major power uses economic and political means to perpetuate or extend its influence over underdeveloped nations or areas.

QUESTIONS TO CONSIDER

1. Why, according to President Johnson, is Vietnam a country that "cannot shape its own destiny"?

2. What promise does Johnson speak of?

3. Why does Ho Chi Minh feel that U.S. military aggression is bound to end in failure?

4. Why does Ho Chi Minh make a distinction between the American people and the American government?

The Terrain of Vietnam

Panorama of Vietnam U.S. Marines move out on the Batangan Peninsula. This panorama depicts the terrain that confronted the troops in Vietnam.

▲

Tall Grass U.S. Marines push their way through the jungle near Make Thieu.

Keeping Watch A U.S. infantryman keeps watch in the Vietnamese jungle. ▶

▲
Calling for Artillery Support U.S. infantrymen prepare for combat near Chu Lai.

◀ **Drop Zone** A U.S. helicopter lifts off after dropping Marines in the jungle.

Jungle War U.S. Marines holed up in a trench.
▼

U.S. Soldiers at War

from

If I Die in a Combat Zone

BY TIM O'BRIEN

On March 8, 1965, the first U.S. unit, the 9th Marine Brigade, landed in Vietnam. They were rapidly followed by seven more battalions, but by the middle of 1965, the military situation in South Vietnam was still worsening. U.S. leaders decided that only a massive influx of combat troops would turn the tide of the war. More and more young American men were called up for service and went off to train for war. Eventually U.S. involvement would grow to more than half-a-million ground troops. In the following excerpt from Tim O'Brien's memoir If I Die in a Combat Zone, *the author describes what it was like to be drafted.*

I was persuaded then, and I remain persuaded now, that the war was wrong. And since it was wrong and since people were dying as a result of it, it was evil. Doubts, of course, hedged all this: I had neither the expertise nor the wisdom to synthesize answers; most of the facts were clouded, and there was no certainty as to the kind of government that would follow a North Vietnamese victory or, for that matter, an American victory, and the specifics of the conflict were hidden away—partly in men's minds, partly in the archives of government, and partly in buried, irretrievable history. The war, I thought, was wrongly conceived and poorly justified. But perhaps I was mistaken, and who really knew, anyway?

Piled on top of this was the town, my family, my teachers, a whole history of the prairie. Like magnets, these things pulled in one direction or the other, almost physical forces weighting the problem, so that, in the end, it was less reason and more gravity that was the final influence.

My family was careful that summer. The decision was mine and it was not talked about. The town lay there, spread out in the corn and watching me, the mouths of old women and Country Club men poised in a kind of eternal readiness to find fault. It was not a town, not a Minneapolis or New York, where the son of a father can sometimes escape scrutiny. More, I owed the prairie something. For twenty-one years I'd lived under its laws, accepted its education, eaten its food, wasted and guzzled its water, slept well at night, driven across its highways, dirtied and breathed its air, wallowed in its luxuries. I'd played on its Little League teams. I remembered Plato's Crito, when Socrates, facing certain death—execution, not war—had the chance to escape. But he reminded himself that he had seventy years in which he could have left the country, if he were not satisfied or felt the agreements he'd made with it were unfair. He had not chosen Sparta or Crete. And, I reminded myself, I hadn't thought much about Canada until that summer.

The summer passed this way. Gold afternoons on the golf course, a comforting feeling that the matter of war would never touch me, nights in the pool hall or drug store, talking with towns-folk, turning the questions over and over, being a philosopher.

Near the end of that summer the time came to go to the war. The family indulged in a cautious sort of Last Supper together, and afterward my father, who is brave, said it was time to report at the bus depot. I moped down to my bedroom and looked the place over, feeling quite stupid, thinking that my mother would come in there in a day or two and probably cry a little. I trudged back up to the kitchen and put my **satchel**[1] down. Everyone gathered around, saying so long and good health and write and let us know if you want anything. My father took up the **induction**[2] papers, checking on times and dates and all the last-minute things, and when I pecked my mother's face and grabbed the satchel for comfort, he told me to put it down, that I wasn't supposed to report until tomorrow.

After laughing about the mistake, after a flush of red color and a flood of ribbing and a wave of relief had come and gone, I took a long drive around the lake, looking again at the place. Sunset Park, with its picnic table and little beach and a brown wood shelter and some families swimming. The Crippled Children's School. Slater Park, more kids. A long string of split-level houses, painted every color.

The war and my person seemed like twins as I went around the town's lake. Twins grafted together and forever together, as if a separation would kill them both.

The thought made me angry.

In the basement of my house I found some scraps of cardboard and paper. With devilish flair, I printed obscene words on them, declaring my intention to have no part of Vietnam. With delightful viciousness, a secret

---

[1] **satchel**—a small bag, often having a shoulder strap.

[2] **induction**—a ceremony or formal act by which a person is inducted, as into office or military service.

will, I declared the war evil, the draft board evil, the town evil in its lethargic acceptance of it all. For many minutes, making up the signs, making up my mind, I was outside the town, I was outside the law, all my old ties to my loves and family broken by the old crayon in my hand. I imagined strutting up and down the sidewalks outside the depot, the bus waiting and the driver blaring his horn, the *Daily Globe* photographer trying to push me into line with the other draftees, the frantic telephone calls, my head buzzing at the deed.

On the cardboard, my strokes of bright red were big and ferocious looking. The language was clear and certain and burned with a hard, defiant, criminal, blasphemous sound. I tried reading it aloud.

Later in the evening I tore the signs to pieces and put the shreds in the garbage can outside, clanging the gray cover down and trapping the messages inside. I went back into the basement. I slipped the crayons into their box, the same stubs of color I'd used a long time before to chalk in reds and greens on Roy Rogers' cowboy boots.

I'd never been a demonstrator, except in the loose sense. True, I'd taken a stand in the school newspaper on the war, trying to show why it seemed wrong. But, mostly, I'd just listened.

"No war is worth losing your life for," a college acquaintance used to argue. "The issue isn't a moral one. It's a matter of efficiency: what's the most efficient way to stay alive when your nation is at war? That's the issue."

But others argued that no war is worth losing your country for, and when asked about the case when a country fights a wrong war, those people just shrugged.

Most of my college friends found easy paths away from the problem, all to their credit. Deferments[3] for this and that. Letters from doctors or chaplains. It was hard

---

[3] deferments—officially sanctioned postponements of compulsory military service.

to find people who had to think much about the problem. Counsel came from two main quarters, pacifists
and veterans of foreign wars.

But neither camp had much to offer. It wasn't a
matter of peace, as the pacifists argued, but rather a
matter of when and when not to join others in making
war. And it wasn't a matter of listening to an ex-
lieutenant colonel talk about serving in a right war, when
the question was whether to serve in what seemed a
wrong one.

On August 13, I went to the bus depot. A
Worthington *Daily Globe* photographer took my picture
standing by a rail fence with four other draftees.

Then the bus took us through corn fields, to little
towns along the way—Lismore and Rushmore and
Adrian—where other recruits came aboard. With some
of the tough guys drinking beer and howling in the back
seats, brandishing their empty cans and calling one
another "scum" and "trainee" and "GI Joe," with all
this noise and hearty farewelling, we went to Sioux
Falls. We spent the night in a Y.M.C.A. I went out alone
for a beer, drank it in a corner booth, then I bought a
book and read it in my room.

By noon the next day our hands were in the air, even
the tough guys. We recited the proper words, some of us
loudly and daringly and others in bewilderment. It was
a brightly lighted room, wood paneled. A flag gave the
place the right colors, there was some smoke in the air.
We said the words, and we were soldiers.

I'd never been much of a fighter. I was afraid of
bullies. Their ripe muscles made me angry: a frustrated
anger. Still, I deferred to no one. Positively lorded myself
over inferiors. And on top of that was the matter of conscience and conviction, uncertain and surface-deep but
pure nonetheless: I was a confirmed liberal, not a paci-
fist; but I would have cast my ballot to end the Vietnam
war immediately, I would have voted for Eugene

McCarthy,[4] hoping he would make peace. I was not soldier material, that was certain.

But I submitted. All the personal history, all the midnight conversations and books and beliefs and learning, were crumpled by **abstention,**[5] extinguished by forfeiture, for lack of oxygen, by a sort of sleepwalking default. It was no decision, no chain of ideas or reasons, that steered me into the war.

---

[4] Eugene McCarthy—In 1968, Eugene Joseph McCarthy (1916–97), a U.S. senator from Minnesota, ran for the Democratic presidential nomination. During his campaign, he called for a negotiated peace in Vietnam. McCarthy's candidacy ended abruptly with the Democratic nomination of Hubert H. Humphrey.

[5] **abstention**—the act of not voting.

QUESTIONS TO CONSIDER

1. Why doesn't O'Brien flee to Canada?

2. How did O'Brien feel during his induction?

3. What is O'Brien most afraid of? Explain your answer.

U.S. Soldiers Arrive

Drafted Air Force inductees prepare to join up.

▲
Here Come the Marines! U.S. Marines arrive at Da Nang
in Vietnam in 1966.

▲

Women at War The first enlisted women in the U.S. Air Force arrive in Vietnam in 1967.

Food A U.S. artilleryman gets a meal while resting on some empty shells. ▶

At Rest U.S. soldiers resting before being transported into the combat zone.
▼

▲
On Call Marines wait to be transported by helicopter into Cam Lo province in 1967.

◀ **Prepared** Members of the 101st Airborne await transport into combat in Vietnam.

Death in the Ia Drang Valley

BY SPECIALIST 4/C JACK P. SMITH

U.S. troops went into action in the summer of 1965 to stabilize the military situation in South Vietnam. Between October 23 and November 20, the U.S. 1st Airmobile Cavalry Division fought a battle with the Viet Cong (the North Vietnamese-backed guerrillas fighting the South Vietnamese government) in the Ia Drang Valley in central South Vietnam. The Viet Cong had entered from Laos with the intention of cutting South Vietnam into two zones. Ia Drang represented a fairly conventional battle between two heavily armed adversaries. Casualties were high, but the Viet Cong were eventually cut off and destroyed. Ia Drang was the only conventional engagement of the Vietnam War. After it, the engagements between the U.S. and the Viet Cong took the form of search-and-destroy missions and attacks on fortified bases. The following is an account of the vicious fighting at Ia Drang, written by a private of the 1st Battalion of the 1st Air Cavalry Division.

The 1st Battalion had been fighting continuously for three or four days, and I had never seen such filthy troops. Some of them had blood on their faces from scratches and from other guys' wounds. Some had long rips in their clothing where shrapnel and bullets had missed them. They all had that look of shock. They said little, just looked around with darting, nervous eyes.

Whenever I heard a shell coming close, I'd duck, but they'd keep standing. After three days of constant bombardment you get so you can tell from the sound how close a shell is going to land within 50 to 75 feet. There were some wounded lying around, bandaged up with filthy shirts and bandages, smoking cigarettes or lying in a coma with plasma bottles hanging above their stretchers.

Late that morning the Cong made a charge. About 100 of them jumped up and made for our lines, and all hell broke loose. The people in that **sector**[1] opened up with everything they had. Then a couple of our Skyraiders came in. One of them dropped a lot of stuff that shimmered in the sun like green confetti. It looked like a ticker-tape parade, but when the things hit the ground, the little pieces exploded. They were antipersonnel[2] charges. Every one of the gooks[3] was killed. Another group on the other side almost made it to the lines. There weren't enough GI's there, and they couldn't shoot them down fast enough. A plane dropped some napalm bombs just in front of the line. I couldn't see the gooks, but I could hear them scream as they burned. A hundred men dead, just like that.

My company, Charlie Company, took over its sector of the battalion perimeter and started to dig in. At three o'clock another attack came, but it never amounted to anything. I didn't get any sleep that night. There was

---

[1] **sector**—a division of an offensive military position.

[2] antipersonnel—designed to inflict death or bodily injury rather than material destruction.

[3] gooks—a derogatory term used during the war to refer to the Vietnamese.

continuous firing from one until four, and it was as bright as day with the flares lighting up the sky.

The next morning the order came for us to move out. I guess our commanders felt the battle was over. The three battalions of PAVN (People's Army of Vietnam—the North Vietnamese) were destroyed. There must have been about 1,000 rotting bodies out there, starting about 20 feet from us and surrounding the giant circle of foxholes. As we left the perimeter, we walked by them. Some of them had been lying out there for four days. There are more ants in Vietnam than in any place I have ever seen.

We were being withdrawn to Landing Zone Albany, some six miles away, where we were to be picked up by helicopter. About noon the column stopped and everybody flopped on the ground. It turned out that our reconnaissance platoon had come upon four sleeping PAVN who had claimed they were deserters. They said that there were three or four snipers in the trees up ahead—friends of theirs who did not want to surrender.

The head of the column formed by our battalion was already in the landing zone, which was actually only 30 yards to our left. But our company was still in the woods and elephant grass. I dropped my gear and my ax, which was standard equipment for supply clerks like me. We used them to cut down trees to help make landing zones for our helicopters. The day had grown very hot. I was about one quarter through a smoke when a few shots cracked at the front of the column.

I flipped my cigarette butt, lay down and grabbed my M-16. The fire in front was still growing. Then a few shots were fired right behind me. They seemed to come from the trees. There was firing all over the place now, and I was getting scared. A bullet hit the dirt a foot to my side, and some started whistling over my head.

This wasn't the three or four snipers we had been warned about. There were over 100 North Vietnamese snipers tied in the trees above us—so we learned later— way above us, in the top branches. The firing kept increasing.

Our executive officer (XO) jumped up and said, "Follow me, and let's get the hell out of here." I followed him, along with the rest of the headquarters section and the 1st Platoon. We crouched and ran to the right toward what we thought was the landing zone. But it was only a small clearing—the L.Z. was to our left. We were running deeper into the ambush.

The fire was still increasing. We were all crouched as low as possible, but still keeping up a steady trot, looking from side to side. I glanced back at Richards, one of the company's radio operators. Just as I looked back, he moaned softly and fell to the ground. I knelt down and looked at him, and he shuddered and started to gurgle deep in his stomach. His eyes and tongue popped out, and he died. He had a hole straight through his heart.

I had been screaming for a medic. I stopped. I looked up. Everyone had stopped. All of a sudden all the snipers opened up with automatic weapons. There were PAVN with machine guns hidden behind every anthill. The noise was deafening.

Then the men started dropping. It was unbelievable. I knelt there staring as at least 20 men dropped within a few seconds. I still had not recovered from the shock of seeing Richards killed, but the jolt of seeing men die so quickly brought me back to life. I hit the dirt fast. The XO was to my left, and Wallace was to my right, with Burroughs to his right. We were touching each other lying there in the tall elephant grass.

Men all around me were screaming. The fire was now a continuous roar. We were even being fired at by our own guys. No one knew where the fire was coming from, and so the men were shooting everywhere. Some were in shock and were blazing away at everything they saw or imagined they saw.

The XO let out a low moan, and his head sank. I felt a flash of panic. I had been assuming that he would get us out of this. Enlisted men may scoff at officers back in the billets,[4] but when the fighting begins, the men automatically become very dependent upon them. Now I felt terribly alone.

The XO had been hit in the small of the back. I ripped off his shirt and there it was: a groove to the right of his spine. The bullet was still in there. He was in a great deal of pain, so a rifleman named Wilson and I removed his gear as best we could, and I bandaged his wound. It was not bleeding much on the outside, but he was very close to passing out.

Just then Wallace let out a "Huh!" A bullet had creased his upper arm and entered his side. He was bleeding in spurts. I ripped away his shirt with my knife and did him up. Then the XO screamed: A bullet had gone through his boot, taking all his toes with it. He was in agony and crying. Wallace was swearing and in shock. I was crying and holding on to the XO's hand to keep from going crazy.

The grass in front of Wallace's head began to fall as if a lawnmower were passing. It was a machine gun, and I could see the vague outline of the Cong's head behind the foot or so of elephant grass. The noise of firing from all directions was so great that I couldn't hear a machine gun being fired three feet in front of me and one foot above my head.

As if in a dream, I picked up my rifle, put it on automatic, pushed the barrel into the Cong's face and pulled the trigger. I saw his face disappear. I guess I blew his head off, but I never saw his body and did not look for it.

Wallace screamed. I had fired the burst pretty close to his ear, but I didn't hit him. Bullets by the thousands were coming from the trees, from the L.Z., from the

---

[4] billets—lodgings for troops.

very ground, it seemed. There was a huge thump near-by. Burroughs rolled over and started a scream, though it sounded more like a growl. He had been lying on his side when a grenade went off about three or four feet from him. He looked as though someone had poured red paint over him from head to toe.

After that everything began getting hazy. I lay there for several minutes, and I think I was beginning to go into shock. I don't remember much.

The amazing thing about all this was that from the time Richards was killed to the time Burroughs was hit, only a minute or two had elapsed. Hundreds of men had been hit all around us, and the sound of men screaming was almost as loud as the firing.

The XO was going fast. He told me his wife's name was Carol. He told me that if he didn't make it, I was to write her and tell her that he loved her. Then he some-how managed to crawl away, saying that he was going to organize the troops. It was his positive decision to do something that reinforced my own will to go on.

QUESTIONS TO CONSIDER

1. How does Private Smith feel about the Viet Cong? Explain.

2. What is the difference between Smith's reaction to the hundreds of Viet Cong killed at Ia Drang and his reaction to the hundreds of U.S. soldiers killed in the ambush?

3. Why does the XO's decision to organize the troops have such a strong effect on Private Smith?

A Journalist Discovers a New Kind of War

BY MICHAEL HERR

Michael Herr (1940–) went to Vietnam in 1967 as a freelance correspondent. Out of his time there came the book Dispatches *(1977), generally cited as the work that best captured the nightmarish tone of life in Vietnam. Herr wrote in a style that fused objective journalism with the rhythms of rock 'n' roll to describe the adrenaline of war. William Burroughs said that in* Dispatches *"All the facades of patriotism, heroism, and the whole colossal fraud of American intervention fall away to the bare bones of fear, war, and death."* Dispatches *is one of the classics accounts of what it is like to be in a war. Herr went on to write the scripts for the Vietnam movies* Apocalypse Now *and* Full Metal Jacket. *The following selection is an excerpt from* Dispatches.

That could be the coldest one in the world, standing at the edge of a clearing watching the chopper you'd just come in on taking off again, leaving you there to think about what it was going to be for you now: if this was a bad place, the wrong place, maybe even the last place, and whether you'd made a terrible mistake this time.

There was a camp at Soc Trang where a man at the lz[1] said, "If you come looking for a story this is your lucky day, we got Condition Red here," and before the sound of the chopper had faded out, I knew I had it too.

"That's affirmative," the camp commander said, "we are *definitely* expecting rain. Glad to see you." He was a young captain, he was laughing and taping a bunch of sixteen clips together bottom to bottom for faster reloading, "grease." Everyone there was busy at it, cracking crates, squirreling away grenades, checking mortar pieces, piling rounds, clicking banana clips into automatic weapons that I'd never even seen before. They were wired into their listening posts out around the camp, into each other, into themselves, and when it got dark it got worse. The moon came up nasty and full, a fat moist piece of decadent fruit. It was soft and saffron-misted[2] when you looked up at it, but its light over the sandbags and into the jungle was harsh and bright. We were all rubbing Army-issue nightfighter cosmetic under our eyes to cut the glare and the terrible things it made you see. (Around midnight, just for something to do, I crossed to the other perimeter and looked at the road running engineer-straight toward Route 4 like a yellow frozen ribbon out of sight and I saw it move, the whole road.) There were a few sharp arguments about who the light really favored, attackers or defenders, men were sitting around with Cinemascope eyes and jaws stuck out like they could shoot bullets, moving and antsing[3] and shifting around inside their

---

[1] lz—landing zone.

[2] saffron-misted—having a strong orange-yellow color.

[3] antsing—fidgeting.

fatigues. "No sense us getting too relaxed, Charlie don't relax, just when you get good and comfortable is when he comes over and takes a giant [expletive] on you." That was the level until morning, I smoked a pack an hour all night long, and nothing happened. Ten minutes after daybreak I was down at the lz asking about choppers.

A few days later Sean Flynn and I went up to a big firebase in the Americal TAOR that took it all the way over to another extreme, National Guard weekend. The colonel in command was so drunk that day that he could barely get his words out, and when he did, it was to say things like, "We aim to make good and [expletive] sure that if *those guys* try *anything cute* they won't catch us with our pants down." The main mission there was to fire H&I, but one man told us that their record was the worst in the whole Corps, probably the whole country, they'd harassed and interdicted a lot of sleeping civilians and Korean Marines, even a couple of American patrols, but hardly any Viet Cong. (The colonel kept calling it "artillerary." The first time he said it Flynn and I looked away from each other, the second time we blew beer through our noses, but the colonel fell in laughing right away and more than covered us.) No sand-bags, exposed shells, dirty pieces, guys going around giving us that look, "We're cool, how come you're not?" At the strip Sean was talking to the operator about it and the man got angry. "Oh *yeah?* Well [expletive] *you*, how tight do you think you want it? There ain't been any veecees around here in three months."

"So far so good," Sean said. "Hear anything on that chopper yet?"

But sometimes everything stopped, nothing flew, you couldn't even find out why. I got stuck for a chopper once in some lost patrol outpost in the Delta where the sergeant chain-ate candy bars and played country-

and-western tapes twenty hours a day until I heard it in my sleep, some sleep, *Up on Wolverton Mountain* and *Lonesome as the bats and the bears in Miller's Cave* and *I fell into a burning ring of fire,* surrounded by strungout rednecks who weren't getting much sleep either because they couldn't trust one of their 400 mercenary troopers or their own hand-packed perimeter guards or anybody else except maybe Baby Ruth and Johnny Cash, they'd been waiting for it so long now they were afraid they wouldn't know it when they finally got it, *and it burns burns burns.* . . . Finally on the fourth day a helicopter came in to deliver meat and movies to the camp and I went out on it, so happy to get back to Saigon that I didn't crash for two days.

* * *

Airmobility, dig it, you weren't going anywhere. It made you feel safe, it made you feel Omni, but it was only a stunt, technology. Mobility was just mobility, it saved lives or took them all the time (saved mine I don't know how many times, maybe dozens, maybe none), what you really needed was a flexibility far greater than anything the technology could provide, some generous, spontaneous gift for accepting surprises, and I didn't have it. I got to hate surprises, control freak at the crossroads, if you were one of those people who always thought they had to know what was coming next, the war could cream you. It was the same with your ongoing attempts at getting used to the jungle or the blow-you-out climate—or the saturating strangeness of the place which didn't lessen with exposure so often as it fattened and darkened in accumulating **alienation.**[4] It was great if you could adapt, you had to try, but it wasn't the same as making a discipline, going into your own reserves and developing a real war metabolism, slow

---

[4] **alienation**—emotional isolation.

yourself down when your heart tried to punch its way through your chest, get swift when everything went to stop and all you could feel of your whole life was the entropy[5] whipping through it. Unlovable terms.

The ground was always in play, always being swept. Under the ground was his, above it was ours. We had the air, we could get up in it but not disappear in to it, we could run but we couldn't hide, and he could do each so well that sometimes it looked like he was doing them both at once, while our finder just went limp. All the same, one place or another it was always going on, rock around the clock, we had the days and he had the nights. You could be in the most protected space in Vietnam and still know that your safety was provisional, that early death, blindness, loss of legs, arms. . . major and lasting disfigurement—the whole rotten deal—could come in on the freakfluky as easily as in the so-called expected ways, you heard so many of those stories it was a wonder anyone was left alive to die in firefights and mortar-rocket attacks. After a few weeks, when the nickel had jarred loose and dropped and I saw that everyone around me was carrying a gun, I also saw that any one of them could go off at any time, putting you where it wouldn't matter whether it had been an accident or not. The roads were mined, the trails booby-trapped, satchel charges and grenades blew up jeeps and movie theaters, the VC got work inside all the camps as shoeshine boys and laundresses and honey-dippers, they'd starch your fatigues and burn your [expletive] and then go home and mortar your area. Saigon and Cholon and Danang held such hostile vibes that you felt you were being dry-sniped every time someone looked at you, and choppers fell out of the sky like fat poisoned birds a hundred times a day. After a

---

[5] entropy—wearing down of matter and energy.

while I couldn't get on one without thinking that I must be out of my [expletive] mind.

Fear and motion, fear and standstill, no preferred cut there, no way even to be clear about which was really worse, the wait or the delivery. Combat spared far more men than it wasted, but everyone suffered the time between contact, especially when they were going out every day looking for it; bad going on foot, terrible in trucks and APC's, awful in helicopters, the worst, traveling so fast toward something so frightening. I can remember times when I went half dead with my fear of the motion, the speed and direction already fixed and pointed one way. It was painful enough just flying "safe" hops between firebases and lz's; if you were ever on a helicopter that had been hit by ground fire your deep, perpetual chopper anxiety was guaranteed. At least actual contact when it was happening would draw long raggedy strands of energy out of you, it was juicy, fast and refining, and traveling toward it was hollow, dry, cold and steady, it never let you alone. All you could do was look around at the other people on board and see if they were as scared and numbed out as you were. If it looked like they weren't you thought they were insane, if it looked like they were it made you feel a lot worse.

I went through that thing a number of times and only got a fast return on my fear once, a too classic hot landing with the heat coming from the trees about 300 yards away, sweeping machine-gun fire that sent men head down into swampy water, running on their hands and knees toward the grass where it wasn't blown flat by the rotor blades, not much to be running for but better than nothing. The helicopter pulled up before we'd all gotten out, leaving the last few men to jump twenty feet down between the guns across the paddy and the gun on the chopper door. When we'd all reached the cover of the wall and the captain had made a check, we were amazed to see that no one had even been hurt, except for one man who'd sprained both his ankles jumping. Afterward, I remembered that I'd been down in the muck worrying about leeches. I guess you could say that I was refusing to accept the situation.

"Boy, you sure get offered some [expletive] choices," a Marine once said to me, and I couldn't help but feel that what he really meant was that you didn't get offered any at all. Specifically, he was just talking about a couple of C-ration cans, "dinner," but considering his young life you couldn't blame him for thinking that if he knew one thing for sure, it was that there was no one anywhere who cared less about what he wanted. There wasn't anybody he wanted to thank for his food, but he was grateful that he was still alive to eat it, that the [expletive] hadn't scarfed him up first. He hadn't been anything but tired and scared for six months and he'd lost a lot, mostly people, and seen far too much, but he was breathing in and breathing out, some kind of choice all by itself.

He had one of those faces, I saw that face at least a thousand times at a hundred bases and camps, all the youth sucked out of the eyes, the color drawn from the skin, cold white lips you knew he wouldn't wait for any of it to come back. Life had made him old, he'd live it out old. All those faces, sometimes it was like looking into faces at a rock concert, locked in, the event had them; or like students who were very heavily advanced, serious beyond what you'd call their years if you didn't know for yourself what the minutes and hours of those years were made up of. Not just like all the ones you saw who looked like they couldn't drag their [expletive] through another day of it. (How do you feel when a nineteen-year-old kid tells you from the bottom of his heart that he's gotten too old for this kind of [expletive]?) Not like the faces of the dead or wounded either, they could look more released than overtaken. These were the faces of boys whose whole lives seemed to have backed up on them, they'd be a few feet away but they'd be looking back at you over a distance you knew you'd never really cross. We'd talk, sometimes fly together, guys going out on R & R,[6] guys escorting bodies, guys who'd flipped over into extremes of peace or violence. Once I flew with a kid who was going home, he looked back down once at the ground where he'd spent the year and spilled his whole load of tears. Sometimes you even flew with the dead.

Once I jumped on a chopper that was full of them. The kid in the op shack[7] had said that there would be a body on board, but he'd been given some wrong information. "How bad do you want to get to Danang?" he'd asked me, and I'd said, "Bad."

When I saw what was happening I didn't want to get on, but they'd made a divert and a special landing for me, I had to go with the chopper I'd drawn, I was afraid of looking squeamish. (I remember, too, thinking that a chopper full of dead men was far less likely to get shot down than one full of living.) They weren't even in bags.[8] They'd been on a truck near one of the firebases in the DMZ[9] that was firing support for Khe Sanh,[10] and the truck had hit a Command-detonated mine, then they'd been rocketed. The Marines were always running out of things, even food, ammo and medicine, it wasn't so strange that they'd run out of bags too. The men had been wrapped around in ponchos, some of them carelessly fastened with plastic straps, and loaded on board. There was a small space cleared for me between one of

---

[6] R & R—abbreviation for rest and relaxation.

[7] op shack—operations shack.

[8] bags—body bags, used for transporting the dead.

[9] DMZ—demilitarized zone.

[10] Khe Sanh—During the first part of the Tet Offensive, the Viet Cong waged a massive attack on the border base of Khe Sanh. ARVN and U.S. troops rushed to Khe Sanh to help defend the base, leaving the major cities of Vietnam vulnerable to Viet Cong attack.

them and the door gunner, who looked pale and so tremendously furious that I thought he was angry with me and I couldn't look at him for a while. When we went up the wind blew through the ship and made the ponchos shake and tremble until the one next to me blew back in a fast brutal flap, uncovering the face. They hadn't even closed his eyes for him.

The gunner started hollering as loud as he could, "Fix it! Fix it!," maybe he thought the eyes were looking at him, but there wasn't anything I could do. My hand went there a couple of times and I couldn't, and then I did. I pulled the poncho tight, lifted his head carefully and tucked the poncho under it, and then I couldn't believe that I'd done it. All during the ride the gunner kept trying to smile, and when we landed at Dong Ha he thanked me and ran off to get a detail.[11] The pilots jumped down and walked away without looking back once, like they'd never seen that chopper before in their lives. I flew the rest of the way to Danang in a general's plane. . . .

When the 173rd held services for their dead from Dak To the boots of the dead men were arranged in formation on the ground. It was an old paratrooper tradition, but knowing that didn't reduce it or make it any less spooky, a company's worth of jump boots standing empty in the dust taking benediction, while the real substance of the ceremony was being bagged and tagged and shipped back home through what they called the KIA Travel Bureau. A lot of the people there that day accepted the boots as solemn symbols and went into deep prayer. Others stood around watching with grudging respect, others photographed it and some just thought it was a lot of bitter [expletive]. All they saw out there was one more set of spare parts, and they wouldn't have looked

---

[11] detail—assignment.

around for holy ghosts if some of those boots filled up again and walked.

Dak To itself had only been the command point for a combat without focus that tore a thirty-mile arc over the hills running northeast to southwest of the small base and airfield there from early November through Thanksgiving 1967, fighting that grew in size and fame while it grew more vicious and out of control. In October the small Dak To Special Forces compound had taken some mortar and rocket fire, patrols went out, patrols collided, companies splintered the action and spread it across the hills in a sequence of small, isolated firefights that afterward were described as strategy; battalions[12] were sucked into it, then divisions, then reinforced divisions. Anyway, we knew for sure that we had a reinforced division in it, the 4th plus, and we said that they had one in it too, although a lot of people believed that a couple of light flexible regiments could have done what the NVA did up and down those hills for three weeks, leaving us to claim that we'd driven him up 1338, up 943, up 875 and 876, while the opposing claims remained mostly unspoken and probably unnecessary. And then instead of really ending, the battle vanished. The North Vietnamese collected up their gear and most of their dead and "disappeared" during the night, leaving a few bodies behind for our troops to kick and count.

"Just like goin' in against the Japs,"[13] one kid called it; the heaviest fighting in Vietnam since the Ia Drang Valley two years before, and one of the only times after Ia Drang when ground fire was so intense that the medevacs couldn't land through it. Wounded backed up for hours and sometimes days, and a lot of men died who might have been saved. Resupply couldn't make it in either, and the early worry about running out of ammunition grew into a panic and beyond, it became real. At the worst, a battalion of Airborne assaulting 875 got caught in an ambush sprung from behind, where no NVA had

---

[12] **battalions**—army units that typically consist of a headquarters and two or more companies, batteries, or similar sub-units.

[13] Japs—derogatory term used to describe the Japanese during World War II.

been reported, and its three companies were pinned and cut off in the raking fire of that trap for two days. Afterward, when a correspondent asked one of the survivors what had happened he was told, "What the [expletive] do you think happened? We got shot to pieces." The correspondent started to write that down and the paratrooper said, "Make that 'little pieces.' We were still shaking the trees for dog tags[14] when we pulled back out of there." Even after the North had gone away, logistics and transport remained a problem. A big battle had to be dismantled piece by piece and man by man. It was raining hard every day now, the small strip at Dak To became overloaded and unworkable, and a lot of troops were shuttled down to the larger strip at Kontum. Some even ended up as far out of their way as Pleiku, fifty miles to the south, for sorting and transport back to their units around II Corps. The living, the wounded and the dead flew together in crowded Chinooks,[15] and it was nothing for guys to walk on top of the half-covered corpses packed in the aisles to get to a seat, or to make jokes among themselves about how funny they all looked, the dumb dead [expletive].

There were men sitting in loose groups all around the strip at Kontum, hundreds of them arranged by unit waiting to be picked up again and flown out. Except for a small sandbagged ops shack and a medical tent, there was no shelter anywhere from the rain. Some of the men had rigged up mostly useless tents with their ponchos, a lot lay out sleeping in the rain with helmets or packs for pillows, most just sat or stood around waiting. Their faces were hidden deep inside the cover of their poncho hoods, white eye movement and silence, walking among them made you feel like you were being watched from hundreds of isolated caves. Every twenty minutes or so a helicopter would land, men would come out or be carried out, others would get on and the chopper would rear up on the strip and fly away, some toward Pleiku and the hospital, others back to the Dak To area and the mop-up operations there. The rotors

---

[14] shaking the trees for dog tags—searching for the dead.

[15] Chinook—a type of helicopter.

of the Chinooks cut twin spaces out of the rain, forcing the spray in slanting jets for fifty yards around. Just knowing what was in those choppers gave the spray a bad taste, strong and briny. You didn't want to leave it on your face long enough to dry.

Back from the strip a fat, middle-aged man was screaming at some troops who were pissing on the ground. His poncho was pulled back away from the front of his helmet enough to show captain's bars, but nobody even turned around to look at him. He groped under his poncho and came up with a .45, pointed it into the rain and fired off a shot that made an empty faraway pop, like it had gone off under wet sand. The men finished, buttoned up and walked away laughing, leaving the captain alone shouting orders to police up[16] the filth; thousands of empty and half-eaten ration cans, soggy clots of Star and Stripes,[17] an M-16 that someone had just left lying there and, worse, evidence of a carelessness unimaginable to the captain, it stank even in the cold rain, but it would police itself in an hour or two if the rain kept up.

---

[16] police up—clean up.

[17] *Star and Stripes*—the newspaper of the U.S. military.

QUESTIONS TO CONSIDER

1. What in Herr's writing best conveys for you a sense of what it was like in Vietnam?

2. What does "expecting rain" mean to the soldiers in Vietnam?

3. What does Herr mean when he says that the U.S. ruled the day and the Viet Cong ruled the night?

4. How would you describe the emotional state of mind of the soldiers in Vietnam?

African Americans in Vietnam

BY THOMAS A. JOHNSON

Because of draft deferments, the brunt of fighting in the Vietnam War fell upon the lower classes of the United States. If you were in college, you could defer going into the army. In practice, this meant that white men from the middle and upper classes—the most likely people to go to college in the U.S. in the 1960s— fought in the war in much smaller numbers than men from the lower classes. African Americans in particular did an inordinate amount of the fighting in Vietnam. As the historian Clark Smith wrote, "Not since the Civil War, when inductees were allowed to buy their exemptions from the national draft, has the burden of military service so directly fallen on a single group of Americans." The following selection is from an article on race relations in Vietnam by Thomas A. Johnson, an African-American correspondent for The New York Times.

SAIGON, South Vietnam—The Army sergeant with the coal-black face muttered: "What in the hell am I doing here? Tell me that—what in the hell am I doing here?"

But there was a smile on his face.

At the moment, he and the men of his under-strength platoon—about half of them Negroes—were crouching on a jungle trail as artillery shells pounded the brush 100 yards away.

At the same time, some 50,000 other Negroes in Vietnam were unloading ships and commanding battalions, walking mountain ranges and flying warplanes, cowering in bunkers and relaxing in Saigon villas.

They were planning battles, moving supplies, baking bread, advising the South Vietnamese Army, practicing international law, patrolling Mekong Delta canals, repairing jets on carriers in the Tonkin Gulf, guarding the United States Embassy, drinking in sleazy bars and dining in the best French restaurants in Saigon, running press centers, digging latrines, driving trucks and serving on the staff of Gen. William C. Westmoreland, the American commander.

They were doing everything and they were everywhere. In this highly controversial and exhaustively documented war, the Negro, and particularly the Negro fighting man, has attained a sudden visibility—a visibility his forefathers never realized while fighting in past American wars.

Fourteen weeks of interviews with black and white Americans serving here reveal that Vietnam is like a speeded-up film of recent racial progress at home. But Vietnam also demonstrates that the United States has not yet come close to solving its **volatile**[1] racial problem.

Why was the sergeant—a 34-year-old career soldier—in Vietnam?

He talked with good humor of the "good Regular Army" to a Negro correspondent, he shuddered with anger recalling that his home-town paper in the Deep South called his parents "Mr. and Mrs." only when

---

[1] **volatile**—explosive.

referring to their hero son, and he pointed out that he had stayed in the Army because his home town offered only "colored" jobs in a clothing factory where whites did the same work for higher pay.

Most often, Negro and white civilians and career soldiers see Vietnam as a **boon**[2] to their careers and as a source of greater income than at home. It was not unusual to hear civilians and career soldiers—Negro and white—express such views as, "Hell, Vietnam's the only war we've got."

For the Negro there is the additional inducement that Southeast Asia offers an environment almost free of discrimination.

One civilian remarked, "Bread and freedom, man, bread and freedom."

To the ordinary Negro fighting man, Vietnam means not only integration but also an integral role in American life—or at least this aspect of American life.

"'The man' can't overlook talent when he wants the job done," said S. Sgt. James Frost, a 29-year-old Negro from Youngstown, Ohio.

In the job of battle, fighting prowess and dependability quickly erase color barriers. Staying alive becomes more important than keeping stateside racial patterns.

During the battle for Hue in February, a knot of white and Negro marines stood knee deep in the mean red mud beside their tank. They were grimy-faced, beard-stubbled and grease-spattered.

They peered across the Huong (Perfume) River, where, more than 300 yards away, unseen North Vietnamese gunners had just given up a mortar and artillery duel.

"They're through for now," said Sgt. Eddie Dailey, a Negro from York, Pa.

---

[2] **boon**—benefit.

"It looks like it," said a white marine with field glasses.

It was 9 A.M., but from somewhere a bottle of liberated Black and White scotch was produced and passed around. "Integration whisky," someone commented. . . .

With the integration of the armed forces in the late nineteen-forties and early fifties, the military quickly outdistanced civilian efforts at breaking down color barriers. This has continued to a point where young Negro men flock to military service for the status, careers and security that many cannot find in civilian life.

A junior infantry officer, who is white, commented:

"It's an awful **indictment**[3] of America that many young Negroes must go into the military for fulfillment, for status—and that they prefer service overseas to their homeland."

The war in Vietnam is filled with ironies, and one of the biggest is that the ordinary Negro fighting man—and especially the teen-age front-line soldier—is not aware of the Negro's participation in previous American wars.

An 18-year-old Marine private at Dongha said proudly: "The brother is here, and he's raising hell. We're proving ourselves."

Officers in Saigon at the headquarters of the Military Assistance Command, Vietnam, say the heavily Negro 173d Airborne Brigade is the best performing unit in Vietnam.

This correspondent went in with the second helicopter wave when the Fourth Battalion of the 173d struck a Vietcong supply base in a thickly forested area of Phuyen Province.

Taking cover in tall grass, he found himself with a young Negro paratrooper, a private first class whose face had not yet sprouted a serious growth of beard.

---

[3] **indictment**—any charge, serious criticism, or cause for blame.

"What you doin' here, bro?" the paratrooper asked. "You gonna do a story on the Fourth Battalion?"

Without waiting for an answer he kept talking.

"You tell them that the 173d is the best [expletive] outfit on this rock. We were the first brigade-size combat unit in Vietnam."

His squad was ordered forward, but he kept talking:

"Tell them we made the first combat jump in Vietnam on Operation Junction City, and that the Fourth Battalion is the best in the 173d. You tell them that—tell them we took Hill 875 at Dakto and that we are steadily kicking Charlie's rear."

Only then did the paratrooper stand up, and as he ran with his squad he called back:

"You tell them, you hear?"

Capt. Robert Fitzgerald, a Harlem-born intelligence officer on General Westmoreland's staff, commented:

"They feel they're the first Negroes to fight because their history books told only of white soldiers, and their movies showed that John Wayne and Errol Flynn won all American wars."

The 31-year-old officer went on: "The only uniform they've seen on Sidney Poitier was a chain-gang suit, and—oh, yes—that of an Army truckdriver once."

Talk of race often leaves white servicemen bored, embarrassed or annoyed. Many say the problem is overly stressed, and many Negro servicemen, especially the teen-aged, first-hitch foot soldiers, say the same thing.

But a Negro sailor stationed in Saigon noted:

"The question of race is always there for the Negro. He would either be blind or insane if it were not. But Vietnam is a buffer or isolation ward to the whole question of race as we know it."

If Vietnam is an isolation ward, then combat is a private room off the ward where the ordinary G.I. can bring to bear the special skill for which he has been trained—killing. And white or black, the G.I.—

usually referred to here as a "grunt" or a "crunch"—is adept at his specialty. The élite units—the airborne, Marines, air cavalry and Special Forces—to which Negro youths flock are among the best of these specialists.

A paratroop officer commented:

"The crunch wants to fight, pure and simple. He's one hell of a fighter, and we couldn't win any war without him because he lives, eats and sleeps to fight. You don't fight wars with gentlemen—that is, you don't win wars with gentlemen."

The grunt is no gentleman.

His average age is 19, and he left high school without finishing. His skills are with the M-16 rifle, the M-60 machine gun, the M-79 grenade launcher, hand grenades and bayonets.

He brags and swears and swaggers, and he runs to a fight. He runs into battle when the first shot is fired, screaming or cursing, as if he does not believe he can be killed.

He can be, however, and he is.

He is killed and wrapped in a green paper blanket and put off to one side until a truck or a helicopter can take him to the rear.

Then he is remembered during quiet times by other young soldiers and marines who still rush into battle, screaming and cursing as if they cannot be killed.

And during those quiet times other things come out.

Like that night in a pitch-black front-line bunker, when it was comforting to hear one another's voices, and the correspondent learned how it was after the Fourth Battalion of the 173d took Hill 875 from a determined enemy force, a force that "had chewed up the Second Battalion."

"We hugged and kissed one another like Girl Scouts, and we cried," said a voice in the darkness.

An Army chaplain comments: "Their anxiousness to prove themselves as men makes them quickly absorb the lesson the military is anxious to teach."

That lesson, an infantry platoon sergeant said, "is to make every man feel that he's in the best army, the best division, the best brigade, the best battalion, the best company, the best platoon, the best squad—and that he's the best [expletive] man in that squad."

And the Negro youngster—from the high-school basketball team, the sharecropper's farm or the riot-ready slums—has consistently volunteered for the élite of the military fighting forces.

"You take a good look at an airborne rifle company and it'll look like there ain't no foreign [white] troops there," one Negro commented.

Dr. Kenneth B. Clark, the Negro psychologist, has noted that a "status not readily available in civilian life" causes Negroes to join the military service at a rate two to three times greater than that for whites, and then to volunteer for élite units.

"There is no chance of asserting his manhood and demonstrating his sense of worth in civilian life," said Dr. Clark, who heads the Metropolitan Applied Research Center in New York. . . .

The Negro makes up 9.8 percent of the military forces in Vietnam, but close to 20 percent of the combat troops and more than 25 percent of such élite Army units as the paratroops. Estimates of Negro participation in some airborne units have been as high as 45 percent, and up to 60 percent of some airborne rifle platoons.

A Negro private first class in the Fourth Battalion of the 173d Airborne Brigade said that when he joined the unit in the summer of 1967 "there were 20 brothers and 8 foreign troops" in his platoon.

About one in every four of the Army's front-line supervisors in the grades of sergeant first class and master sergeant is a Negro, a fact attesting to the higher

Negro re-enlistment rate in the armed forces in general and the Army in particular.

The re-enlistment rate for first-term Army men in 1965 was 49.3 percent for Negroes and 13.7 percent for whites; in 1966 the figures were 66.5 and 20.0. Re-enlistment figures for 1967 have not been completed, a Pentagon spokesman said. Generally, the rate in the Army runs at least three times as high as for whites, and in the other services two times as high.

The present Negro death rate in Vietnam is 14.1 percent of total American fatalities; for 1961 to 1967 it was 12.7 percent. Late in 1965 and early in 1966 the Negro death rate soared to about 25 percent, and the Pentagon ordered a cut-back in front-line participation by Negroes.

It is in the front lines that commonly shared adversity has always sprouted quickly into group loyalty and brotherhood. And whether between white and white, Negro and Negro, or Negro and white, Vietnam is no exception to the tradition of battlefield brotherhood.

"The stereotypes they had believed just sort of melt away," said Capt. Richard Traegerman, a 25-year-old West Pointer from Philadelphia. "Whites see Negroes are as intelligent and brave as anyone else, and Negroes see whites are just guys with the same strengths and weaknesses as anyone else."

A Negro soldier said he felt that the Negro underwent more of a change than the white.

"The Negro sees the white boy—really sees him— for the first time," he said. "He's just another dude without all those things to back him up and make him bigger than he is—things like a police department, big job or salary."

And a long-time front-line observer said:

"It's the most natural thing in the world to come out closer than brothers after a few days on the line. Up here it's a real pleasure to just be warm and dry or to feel a cool breeze; to have fresh water, a heat cube for C rations; to wash or take off your shoes or to be alive when others are dying. This will make any two people brothers."

For the most part, Negroes in Vietnam say that the closest thing to real integration that America has produced exists here.

"It's the kind of integration that could kill you, though," a Negro sailor remarked.

There are reports of racial discrimination, racial fights and instances of self-segregation, but most Negroes interviewed said these instances were greatly outweighed by racial cooperation.

In effect, while participating in a war that pits yellow people against yellow people, America is demonstrating that its black and white people can get along.

QUESTIONS TO CONSIDER

1. Why did many African-American soldiers in Vietnam assume they were the first blacks to fight in a U.S. war?

2. Was race an important issue in Vietnam? Explain.

3. According to Johnson, why did African-American soldiers consistently volunteer for the élite units?

4. How did African-American soldiers feel about their white counterparts?

On Patrol

Single File U.S. Marines on patrol in a rice paddy.

▲
Airlift U.S. infantrymen are airlifted to a new staging area during a search-and-destroy mission near Chu Chi in 1966.

◀ **Firepower** A U.S. soldier moves away from a village being hit by mortars.

▲

Capturing Viet Cong Marines escort two Viet Cong prisoners out of the jungle.

What They Carried Paratroopers on patrol in Phuoc Tuy province in 1966. ▶

▲
Relieving the Heat Marines try to cool off in a stream.

from

A Piece of My Heart

BY KEITH WALKER

A great deal of oral history of the war has been recorded by interviewers and journalists. Keith Walker's book A Piece of My Heart *(1985) contains the stories of twenty-six women who served in Vietnam, presenting a perspective on the war often left out of the military histories. Maureen Walsh served as nurse in the U.S. Navy. In 1968 she was sent to Vietnam and worked in a hospital at Da Nang, on the coast. On a regular basis, she was responsible for caring for more than three hundred patients. Walsh's fiancé, a marine pilot, was killed while they were both serving in Vietnam. The following is Walsh's account of working in the hospital at Da Nang.*

The first two nights I was there we didn't have any incoming or anything, though we could hear it in the peripheral areas. But my introduction to Vietnam nursing was on the third night as I was walking outside, going from one building to the next, checking the patients— and I was feeling overwhelmed as it was. From the mountains behind us, the Viet Cong were sending in mortars and rockets, and I heard this tremendous roar go over my head. I never heard a rocket in my life. I didn't know whether it was a plane, or a helicopter—I couldn't imagine what it was. Phew! This red, flaming thing came flying over, and I thought, "Oh, my God, that thing's from outer space." Well, when I heard that whoosh I went into one of the bunkers, and I know that I did not reach the bottom, because I felt all this stuff crawling around down there. I think I hit bottom and bounced right back out. I knew they were rats; they had to be rats! I said to myself, "Dear God, am I going to get bit by a rat and have to go home, or am I going to get hit by the shrapnel up here?" I decided it would be more honorable to be hit by the shrapnel, such a choice! So I just kind of buried into the sidewalk, and as I was kissing the concrete I looked up to watch all of this action. As I turned my head to the right—we were sort of on a hill on a sand dune—I could see the Marine base receiving rockets. As they went in I could see the planes explode. . . this was like a movie! I couldn't conceive that I was really there. I was a participant, but I still didn't feel like I was going to get hit, because I really wasn't there; it was total denial.

Finally, everything stopped and I didn't know whether to get up. Navy nurses wore white uniforms over there, and we were walking targets. The Vietnamese village—we called it "the vill"—the Viet Cong vill was right behind us. Often times our people would take sniper[1] fire at night. I didn't know about the sniper fire—that came a few days later—but I took my white hat off. If I had had something to put around me I would've, because I knew instinctively I was a sitting duck out there. So I just got up and said, "Well, I guess I'm in Vietnam, and I've got to do the best I can," looked down to make sure I hadn't wet my pants, went on to

---

[1] sniper—a skilled military shooter detailed to spot and pick off enemy soldiers from a concealed place.

the next building, and walked into the ward. Some of my corpsmen had been there six or seven months, and this was a routine night to them. I must've looked as white as my uniform, and they started laughing as I came into the unit. They started teasing me about getting into a little action already. I could've clobbered them. So I guess I got my initiation; that was it. I was frightened as hell, and I was excited, yet on the other hand, if I let the emotions run away with me, I would've been totally **incapacitated.**[2]

As it was, I was fighting inexperience; my former chief nurse was right. I was really flying by the seat of my pants as far as going into these units and checking the patients. To make up for my inexperience, I'd read the chart, check all the IVs, dressings, and casts several times for each patient. Each person had enough "plumbing" to make the average plumber marvel. I mean, there were machines on every person—suction, respirators, monitors of all sorts—everybody had multiple intravenous fluids infusing, catheters,[3] and all sorts of **sundry**[4] tubes and drains. By the time you weed through that to find the poor individual under it all, you couldn't really make him out. It was incredible!

I really had to stifle the emotions in order to be able to focus in on what was happening to each and every one of those patients and to keep all of that data in mind, write everything down, as well as talk to all of the corpsmen. I didn't even know all of the corpsmen at that point; I didn't know all of the patients. I would hope and pray every time I would leave a unit to go to the next one that I wouldn't find so much devastation, because already I was overwhelmed from the other wards. But I found similar situations on every ward. I think I had five wards that were my responsibility. And that's what we

---

[2] **incapacitated**—overcome; disabled.

[3] catheters—medical devices that permit injection or withdrawal of fluids.

[4] **sundry**—various.

did when we worked the night shift. I had so much responsibility and so much to do on each of the units that I couldn't worry about the extraneous goings on outside.

Nights were especially difficult because this was the time when people who were wounded would be very frightened—moaning and groaning and calling out. Marines were incredibly stoic. It was surprising that they didn't cry out more than they did. There were a lot of times when they died on us at night. I mean, I would go from one unit to the next and have three, four, five Marines die maybe in the period of one night. Some of them in my arms. I'd be holding them, and they'd be hanging on— "Oh, I don't want to die!" You have to say, "Well, God, I can't get involved, I can't get involved," but it's pretty damn hard not getting involved when you see a nineteen- or twenty-year-old blond kid from the Midwest or California or the East Coast screaming and dying. A piece of my heart would go with each! You knew that their families would be getting a visit from the Marine Corps two days later. It was all I could do to hold back the tears, and we did hold back a lot, which I think was very unhealthy. It started very early; we had no way to really let loose with each other. One of the things we found is that we were all so extremely busy that we didn't have time to let loose with each other. The other aspect was that there was some sort of a feeling with nurses at the time that we were all volunteers that went over there. Since we were volunteers, we had to take what we got and not complain about it. The "shut up and do your work" mentality. . . .

I want to talk about the intensive care unit. The other units were nothing compared with what the intensive care units were like. Many times when we were on duty and there were a lot of casualties coming in, the doctors would necessarily be taken to the triage area.[5] That left the nurses and the corpsmen to do the best we could on the units. We couldn't call the doctors to

---

[5] triage area—place where wounded soldiers are sorted and treated.

do some of the things that were physician-related. For instance, patients would pop bleeders on the ward; they would start bleeding under their dressings. What we would have to do is make decisions about . . . We'd have to go in and clamp off bleeders. And it was rather a touchy situation because, you know, it looks pretty clear when you're in the laboratory or the operating room, but if you're not a surgeon, it's pretty hard to tell one artery from a ureter. It was anxiety-producing, to say the least.

Several times when we would have incoming, the mortars would blow out our regular and emergency generators. Of about twenty patients in the ICU, there were usually ten to fifteen on respirators, with chest tubes, and when the electricity went off, you can just imagine what chaos ensued. We often had to do mouth-to-mouth or trach-to-trach breathing for these people until the emergency power came on. We would have a few ambubags.[6] We'd be throwing them around like footballs from one end of the unit to the other. So we lost people that way too. It was so frustrating, and a lot of times we'd have to give up breathing because we were so exhausted we would have passed out. That happened four or five times when I was on duty.

One night I was walking through one of the units that was right off the helicopter pad, when a mortar came in and exploded. Shrapnel came in the door—went right by me, under my legs. Another piece came in as I was count-ing narcotics for one of the corpsmen at the medicine cabinet near the door. The shrapnel went through his eye and through his head, went through the medicine cabinet, exited through the unit on the other side, and lodged in the wall. God, that was awful, that was awful to see that.

Another night that we had some incoming, we were walking along the walkway and I saw one of the mortars hit smack-dead on one of our units; it exploded. There was not a lot of screaming and yelling, but mostly what really

---

[6] ambubags—name for a kind of medical equipment used for resuscitation.

hit me was the stench, the burning flesh. The Marines never screamed, which is incredible, their training is incredible. I remember going into the ward. The lights were all out, so I couldn't see a thing, but we knew there was a lot of activity. I'm not so sure I would've been prepared to see immediately what was happening. I had a flashlight with me . . . opened the flashlight and there was just chunks of flesh and blood all over the wall. Wounded men had been wounded again in the unit. Four of our corpsmen were killed that night. One of our nurses that was out going from one unit to another got down just in time. The way the shrapnel came it would've decapitated[7] her had she not been down. I don't know how any of our nurses missed getting hit—by some miracle.

There were times when, as I say, the doctors weren't immediately available, and we had to make major life-saving decisions. One night, as a typical example, I was on a neurosurgery unit. We had a lot of casualties, and the doctors were all tied up in triage. I had a young man that was put on the unit, and the doctor said, "You've got to do the best you can with him." As soon as the doctor left, he went into respiratory distress, and I had to do a tracheostomy[8] on him, and God, there was no equipment on the unit to do something like that—most of our patients went to the operating room to have something like that done. I just had to put a slit in his throat, and all I had was a ball-point pen; I had to unscrew that and put the tube of the pen into the trachea, which is a common thing actually—it's the only thing you had on you. There were a lot of those kinds of things going on that we had to do, things that we were never taught.

I'll never forget this one night. I was sitting next to this bed, and a young corpsman came in . . . and I looked at his name, of course. I had known him in the States. He was one of the fellows that was at the naval

---

[7] decapitated—cut off the head of.

[8] tracheostomy—surgical opening made in the neck to allow the passage of air into the trachea.

air station with me, but when I had seen him, I didn't recognize him because his wounds were so severe and numerous. There's no way you can save somebody like that, but the most incredible thing is that he was clear—he was talking with me; he knew who I was. I was holding the one hand that he had left, and as I was talking with him, he said, "I know I'm not going to live." . . . I remember him telling me to contact his mother, and he was telling me how much he enjoyed our friendship, and he said, "Please don't leave me." This young man was losing blood at a tremendously quick rate, and what amazed me is that he was still so clear. He grabbed my hand and I talked to him for as long as possible, and I just felt that grip loosening and loosening and loosening. The only thing I could do was sit there and pray with him. I knew he was going to leave this holocaust; he was lucky. I just told him good-bye.

Many times I'd have fellows that would come in the ward—especially the Navy corpsmen, some of whom I had trained—and some of them had been stationed with me at the units back at Quonset Point. That was horrible, seeing those men come in wounded. They were just like brothers to us, because the Navy nurses and the Navy corpsmen and the Corps WAVES[9] had a very close bond. We worked very very closely and went through a great deal together. You knew their families, where they came from—you knew everything about them. And to see them come in—they were just like having your own family, own brothers, get killed. Those are some of the memories in the intensive care unit.

---

[9] WAVES—an acronym for women in the naval service.

QUESTIONS TO CONSIDER

1. Why were nights in particular so difficult for the nurses?
2. What did Maureen Walsh find most stressful about her job as a front line-nurse?
3. What did she find most rewarding?

Letters Home

EDITED BY BERNARD EDELMAN

There is no better way to understand what the war was like for U.S. soldiers than to read their letters. Sent to loved ones and family members, these letters describe the way soldiers felt and what they thought they were doing far better than any historian could hope to. William Broyles wrote in the foreword to the collection Dear America, *"As I read the letters in this book I could see the men I served with in Vietnam fifteen years ago, their faces dirty and sweaty and plastered with big grins that hid the fear. And I could hear the true voices of Vietnam again—not filtered by the media, not smoothed out in recollection, but direct, raw, personal: the way it was." The letters in the following selection are from* Dear America: Letters Home From Vietnam *(1985), compiled by Bernard Edelman from a collection made by the New York Vietnam Veterans Memorial Commission. Each letter is followed by a brief biographical sketch of the author.*

Dec. 23, 1966

Dear Mom and Dad,

Everything is just fine—in fact it's better than I thought it would be. They have us in a big base camp.

We're going to be staying here for a month. This area is perfectly safe. While we're in base camp, we aren't allowed to carry ammo or even keep it in our tents. . . .

Besides the platoon leader, I'm the next most important man in the platoon. All the talk I hear from the guys who have been here awhile make it sound pretty easy over here. We eat three hot meals a day. I heard when we go to the field, they fly hot meals to us in the morning and night, and for lunch you eat C-rations, and you're allowed two canteens of water a day. When you're in home base you drink all you want, plus while you're in the field you get a beer and soda free every other day.

Last night I had a little trouble falling asleep because of the artillery rounds going off. It's a 175 [mm gun], and it has a range of miles, but when it goes off it sounds like a firecracker going off in your ear. All in all things look pretty good. They have PX's where you can buy whatever you want or need, which is doing me no good because I'm broke. Don't send me money because it's no good here. We use scrip for money which looks like a Sweepstakes ticket, and besides I'll be getting paid in a few days. You should be receiving a $150 in about a week. If you need it, you can use it, but if you don't, then put it in a bank, OK?

The people live like pigs. They don't know how to use soap. When they have to go to the bathroom, they go wherever they're standing, they don't care who is looking. Kids not even six [years old] run up to you and ask for a cig. The houses they live in are like rundown shacks. You can see everything—they have no doors, curtains. I'm real glad I have what I have. It seems poor to you maybe, and you want new things because you think our house doesn't look good, but after seeing the way these people live, there's no comparison. We are more than millionaires to these people—they have nothing. I can't see how people can live like this. It seems funny, in one of your letters you write about the TV going on the blink. At the same time, I almost had to laugh. These people don't even have the slightest idea what a TV is even.

Right now our big guns are going off and it sounds good knowing it's yours and they don't have any. . . .

It takes me a day to write one letter, and every chance I have I'd rather write to you than anyone else. Tell Susan I'm sorry, but I just don't have the time to write as much as I would like to. . . . Mom, the least of my problems now are girls. That's one of the things I don't have time to worry about.

One thing I don't do is worry—it doesn't pay. If I worried about everything over here that there is to worry about, I'd have a nervous breakdown. I'm very fortunate, because I have a cool head. Things that make other guys scared or shaky don't seem to bother me. Also I'm fortunate because my platoon leader, Lt. Sanderson, also keeps a cool head. This man is really sharp when it comes to this stuff. I have already learned a lot about human nature from this man. He's only 23 years old, but his knowledge is really something. A person can't go wrong following his example.

Well, it's about time. I thought you would never send those onions. I can't wait for them to arrive. . . .

For sure, now, I'm going to close this short novel.

With all my love,
Your grateful son,
Johnny

On 2 February 1967, less than two months after he arrived in country, PFC John Dabonka was killed in action near the Mekong Delta town of My Tho. He was 20 years old.

* * *

Dear Madeline,

Hello my dear sister.

Boy, I sure feel close to you. Since your last letter, I almost feel as if you are my sister. It's good to have someone to tell your troubles to. I can't tell them to my parents or Darlene because they worry too much, but I tell you truthfully I doubt if I'll come out of this alive.

In my original squad I'm the only one left unharmed. In my platoon there's only 13 of us. It seems every day another young guy 18 and 19 years old like myself is killed in action. Please help me, Mad. I don't know if I should stop writing my parents and Darlene or what.

I'm going on an operation next month where there is nothing but V C and V C sympathizers. The area is also very heavily mined. All of us are scared cause we know a lot of us won't make it. I would like to hear what you have to say about it, Madeline, before I make any decisions.

Oh, and one more favor. I'd like the truth now. Has Darlene been faithful to me? I know she's been dating guys, but does she still love me best? Thanks for understanding. See ya if it's God's will. I have to make it out of Vietnam though, cause I'm lucky. I hope. Ha ha.

Miss ya,
Love,
Ray

PFC Raymond C. Griffths went to Vietnam just after Christmas in 1965 and was assigned to Company A, 1st Battalion, 9th Marines, 3rd Marine Division. He wrote this letter to Madeline Velasco, a friend from high school in San Francisco, California, in June 1966. He was killed a few weeks later, on the Fourth of July. He was 19 years old.

6 Dec. '69
1230 hr.

Dear Gail:

Hi, doll. How's my girl today? I hope you are not feeling too blue. Well, we are on the move again. We got the word to pack our stuff, and we are going to Ban Me Thuot. We are not going to the village itself, but to the airfield. I think we are going to guard the airfield for a while. From what we have heard, we can get showers there and we can even get sodas or beer. Boy, we have not had anything cold to drink in a long time. It does get us mad that we have to move again. We just got our bunkers built—it took us about 1,000 sandbags to build [them]—and now some other company is coming in and using them. That's the way it seems to be all the time. We do all the hard work and then we have to move. Well, that's the Army for you.

I remember in one of your letters you said you were surprised that I said I don't mind being here. Well in a way, that's true. Sure I want to be home with you and have all the things we dream about. But yet being here makes a man feel proud of himself—it shows him that he is a man. Do you understand? Anyone can go in the Army and sit behind a desk, but it takes a lot to do the fighting and to go through what we have to. When we go home, we can say, "Yes, I was in Vietnam. Yes, I was a line dog." To us it means you have gone to hell and have come back. This is why I don't mind being here, because we are men. . . .

Love,
Pete

Sp/4 Peter H. Roepcke, from Glendale, New York, served as a "line dog"—an infantryman—with Company A, 3rd Battalion, 506th Infantry, 101st Airborne Division, from September 1969 until April 1970, operating in I Corps, when he broke his leg while jumping from a helicopter. He died of a heart attack in October 1981.

* * *

March 2 [1969]

Darling,

I love you so very, very much. Finally it's over for a while and I can write. I don't know where to begin or what to say or how. I guess I'll just try to tell you how I feel, which is mostly proud, sad, tired and relieved. After all these endless days and nights, they gave me and the platoon 36 hours off. I spent today going to memorial services for my people, doing wash, catching up on work in my office and writing up people for medals.

Oh, Darling, it's been so unreal. I'm not going to go into detail—it would only scare, depress or worry you. Just be convinced I'm fine, it's over and all I have to complain of now is a bad cold and a lot of fatigue. These last days were just so filled with fighting, marching, thinking, all the time thinking, "Am I doing it right? Is this what they said at Quantico?[1] How can I be sure I haven't led us into a trap and the NVA are waiting?" etc., etc., until I became so exhausted just by worrying. I'm just so grateful (to whom?). I "only" lost six men (I know how awful that sounds)! I had a seventh guy fall off a cliff and get a bad cut and concussion, but he'll be OK.

I'm so confused. At the services today they were talking about God protecting people and eternal life and

---

[1] Quantico—military training camp.

I felt so **desolate,**[2] so despairing. I know there is no reward waiting for them or any hope. I began crying I felt so awful and hopeless, but somehow held it back and it just looked like I was sniffling from my cold. (See! How awful my ego and pride that I couldn't even let myself weep for those poor, poor kids!) All I can say is that considering how awful it was, I'm so lucky I didn't lose more.

I said I was proud. Mostly of them. I'm putting 10 of them in for decorations. Enclosed are some of the rough drafts of citations. Don't read them if you don't want to. Just save them for me. I guess I should be honest. I've been nominated, I hear, for the Silver Star, the third highest medal. Please don't get upset. I didn't try to win it—I was just trying to keep my people alive and doing the best I could. I may not even get it, 'cause the reviewing board might knock it down to a Bronze Star. You know me so well, you know I'm lying if I say I'm not pleased. I am, I'm proud, but only the worst part of me. My better part is just so sad and unhappy this whole business started.

Again, though it may be foolish, I'll keep my word and be honest. The post-Tet offensive[3] isn't over. All intelligence points to a return bout. However, my platoon is 1,000% better than it was, we have so much support now—like a family, really. We'll all watch out for each other. Also, we don't believe they'll hit again near here, so whatever happens, I'll be OK. That's the truth too, honey. I have fantastic good luck, as strange as that may sound, and what's US is too good and too strong for any badness.

Love,
Brian

---

[2] **desolate**—bereft of friends or hope; sad and forlorn.
[3] Tet offensive—see pages 228–236.

Brian Sullivan, a lieutenant assigned to the 4th Battalion, 11th Regiment, 1st Marine Division, was a field artillery officer and infantry platoon commander in the area around Da Nang from June 1968 to June 1969. He is now an associate professor of history at Yale University and lives in New York City. This letter was written to his then-wife Tobie.

* * *

19 October 67

Mom and Dad—

Your oldest son is now a captain in the United States Marine Corps. I was promoted yesterday. Of all the men selected for captain, 1,640 men, only about 50 men have been promoted to date. I was one of the 50, to my surprise and pleasure. My effective date of rank is 1 July 1967, which means I have technically been a captain for 3½ months. I am thus due back pay for 3½ months. With this promotion, my annual income is $9,000.00 a year. I'm single, 24 years old, college-educated, a captain in the Marine Corps, and I have $11,000.00 worth of securities. That is not a bad start in life, is it?

As I understand, Dad, you were married about this point in life. There was a war going on then too. I really know very little about those years in my parents' lives. Sometime you will have to tell me about them—what you were doing, what you were thinking, what you were planning, what you were hoping.

Mom, I appreciate all your letters. I appreciate your concern that some of the things you write about are trivial, but they aren't trivial to me. I'm eager to read anything about what you are doing or the family is doing. You can't understand the importance these "trivial" events take on out here. It helps keep me civilized. For a while, as I read your letters, I am a normal person. I'm not killing people, or worried about being killed. While I read your letters, I'm not carrying guns and grenades. Instead I am going ice skating with David or walking through a department store to exchange a lamp shade. It is great to know your family's safe, living in a secure country; a country made secure by thousands upon thousands of men who have died for that country.

In the Philippines I took a bus ride along the infamous route of the death march in Bataan. I passed graveyards that were marked with row after row after row of plain white crosses. Thousands upon thousands. These were American graves—American graves in the Philippines. And I thought about the American graves in Okinawa, Korea, France, England, North Africa—around the world. And I was proud to be an American, proud to be a Marine, proud to be fighting in Asia. I have a commitment to the men who have gone before me, American men who made the sacrifices that were required to make the world safe for ice skating, department stores and lamp shades.

No, Mom, these things aren't trivial to me. They are vitally important to me. Those are the truly important things, not what I'm doing. I hope you will continue to write about those "trivial" things because that is what I enjoy learning about the most.

Your son,
Rod

In September 1968, Capt. Rodney R. Chastant, from Mobile, Alabama, extended his 13-month tour of duty in Vietnam with Marine Air Group 13, 1st Marine Air Wing, Da Nang. He was killed on 22 October. He was 25 years old. David is his brother.

* * *

May 19, 1968

Dear Mom and Dad,

How is everyone? I hope fine. When you receive this letter, May will be just about over. I will be down to six months and a couple of days left in December which amounts to nothing. I'm going to have a big celebration when I leave Vietnam. And when I get back to the World, I won't forget to keep the seventh day open to the Lord.

I guess the time is passing by fairly fast for you, because you're pretty busy. "But not for me." Received all your letters, Ma, and I'm always glad to hear from a squared-away mother, as the Army would say it about a Number 1 soldier. It all just comes to the heading— you're the best in my books, Ma.

Also heard from Aunt Flo. I know you will thank her for me, about writing to me, it was nice of her. So far you're doing good, Ma, about writing. Keep up the good work. Now I want to let you know you will always be Number 1 mother in my books.

Heard you got Nancy a portable hair dryer. I think it was nice of you to always look out for the other person. But, remember, stay like you are, and don't let them take advantage of a well-natured mother. Also, keep up the good work, and keep the letters flowing in. Say hi to everyone.

Love,
Rick

P.S. Watch my return address. I'm all over— everywhere.

Sp/4 Richard A. Carlson, a medic attached to Company D, 2nd Battalion, 8th Cavalry, 1st Cavalry Division (Airmobile), operating in I Corps, had been in Vietnam four months when he was killed while ministering to the wounded during an ambush on 24 May 1968. "Doc, I'm a mess," he said to a fellow medic. "Oh, God, I don't want to die. Mother, I don't want to die. Oh, God, don't let me die." These were his last words. He was 20 years old.

QUESTIONS TO CONSIDER

1. Why do you think Lt. Sullivan feels guilty for earning a Silver Star?

2. Why does Captain Chastant enjoy "trivial" news from home?

3. What emotions do some or all of these soldiers have in common?

Poetry

BY BRUCE WEIGL, W. D. EHRHART, AND YUSEF KOMUNYAKAA

Bruce Weigl is a veteran of the First Air Cavalry who has published three collections of poetry. "Mines" describes one of the most horrific hazards faced by U.S. soldiers in Vietnam. W. D. Ehrhart edited Demilitarized Zones *(1976), the first collection of poetry by Vietnam veterans. His poem "The Next Step," like "Mines," deals with the fear faced by soldiers out on patrol. Yusef Komunyakaa's* Dien Cai Dau *(1988) is one of the most important collections of poems published about the Vietnam War. Already a renowned poet, this collection represented the first time Komunyakaa chose to write about his Vietnam experiences. "Somewhere Near Phu Bai" is about being out on patrol, and "Roll Call" describes the funeral of some fellow soldiers.*

Mines

BY BRUCE WEIGL

1

In Vietnam I was always afraid of mines:
North Vietnamese mines, Vietcong mines,
French mines, American mines,
whole fields marked with warning signs.

A Bouncing Betty comes up waist high—
    cuts you in half.
One man's legs were laid
alongside him in the Dustoff,
he asked for a chairback, morphine,
he screamed he wanted to give
his eyes away, his kidneys,
his heart . . .

2

Here is how you walk at night: slowly lift
one leg, clear the sides with your arms, clear the back,
front, put the leg down, like swimming.

The Next Step

BY W.D. EHRHART

The next step you take
may lead you into an ambush.

The next step you take
may trigger a tripwire.

The next step you take
may **detonate**[1] a mine.

The next step you take
may split your belly open.

The next step you take
may send a sniper's bullet through your brain.

The next step you take.
The next step you take.

The next step.
The next step.

The next step.

Roll Call

BY YUSEF KOMUNYAKAA

Through rifle sights
we must've looked like crows
perched on a fire-eaten branch
lined up for reveille[2] ready
to roll-call each M-16
propped upright
between a pair of jungle boots,

---

[1] **detonate**—to explode or cause to explode.

[2] reveille—bugle call or roll call in a camp or garrison.

a helmet on its barrel
as if it were a man.
The perfect row aligned
with the chaplain's cross
while a metallic-gray squadron
of sea gulls circled. Only
a few lovers have blurred
the edges of this picture.
Sometimes I can hear them
marching through the house,
closing the distance. All
the lonely beds take me back
to where we saluted those
five pairs of boots
as the sun rose against our faces.

Somewhere Near Phu Bai

BY YUSEF KOMUNYAKAA

The moon cuts through
night trees like a circular saw
white hot. In the guard shack
I lean on the sandbags,
taking aim at whatever.
Hundreds of blue-steel stars
cut a path, fanning out
silver for a second. If anyone's
there, don't blame me.

I count the shapes ten meters
out front, over & over, making sure
they're always there.
I don't dare blink an eye.
The white-painted backs
of the Claymore mines
like quarter-moons.
They say Victor Charlie[3] will
paint the other sides & turn
the blast toward you.

If I hear a noise
will I push the button
& blow myself away?
The moon grazes treetops.
I count the Claymores again.
Thinking about buckshot
kneaded in the plastic C-4
of the brain, counting
sheep before I know it.

---

[3] Victor Charlie—Viet Cong.

QUESTIONS TO CONSIDER

1. What do you think is the poet's message in "The Next Step"?

2. What emotions does Yusef Komunyakaa express in his poetry?

3. Which of these poems best helped you understand what it was like to be a soldier in Vietnam? Explain.

Combat

Attack U.S. infantry assault a Viet Cong position after an
artillery barrage.

▲

Artillery U.S. soldiers fire a 105mm howitzer in support of infantry. This was the main artillery piece used by the U.S. Army in Vietnam.

Captured Target A destroyed Viet Cong base camp with a U.S. Marine in front holding a recoilless rifle. ▶

◀ **His War Is Over** Two soldiers carry a wounded comrade to a helicopter so he can be airlifted out.

Helping the Wounded U.S. soldiers carry a wounded comrade though the jungle.
▼

The Vietnamese
at War

Joining the Viet Cong

BY SUSAN SHEEHAN

Viet Cong (VC) was originally a term used to describe Communist troops that went underground in South Vietnam after the Geneva Conference (see pages 16–23), but the term quickly came to apply to the rapidly expanding Communist guerrilla movement in the South. This guerrilla movement often forcibly recruited its troops from the villages of South Vietnam, subjecting these "draftees" to intensive indoctrination and political education. The following selection is an account of Huynh Van Kim, who joined the Viet Cong in 1957 and served for eight years before escaping in 1965. In Susan Sheehan's book Ten Vietnamese *(1967), Kim explained what life was like as a VC and why he left.*

Huynh Van Kim, who has also used the aliases Huynh Thanh and Huynh Long, joined the Viet Cong in January, 1958, when it was still known as the underground revolutionary movement. He was then twenty-one years old.

One night in December, 1957, a dozen Viet Cong recruiting agents appeared in his hamlet in Binh Thuan village, in the delta province of Dinh Tuong. Some of the agents, who were dressed as Viet Minh troops, were armed. They invited Kim and five or six other young men in the hamlet to accompany them to a base in the jungle a mile away. Kim was afraid and said he wouldn't go, but the agents told him they just wanted to have a friendly talk with him and he consented to follow them. Once at their base, the agents lectured the boys. The lectures pointed out some of the shortcomings of Diem's régime—his failure to hold the agreed-upon 1956 elections, to carry out land reform, or to remove corrupt officials. The young men were urged to join the revolutionary movement in order to work for Diem's overthrow. The agents said that this would result in justice for the people, a more equitable distribution of land, and reunification of the country. After a couple of hours, the agents let the boys go, warning them to say nothing about their activities. The agents returned every night. Each time they came to the hamlet they invited five or six young men to go with them. They came to Kim's home and invited him to lectures every third or fourth night. The agents kept asking him if he had made a decision to join the movement. At the end of a month of lectures, Kim agreed to join.

Kim, who is now a well-built, high-strung, chain-smoking young man of twenty-nine with watchful eyes, a forced smile, and a nervous habit of cracking his knuckles, joined the Viet Cong for several reasons. He was favorably impressed by the VC indoctrination lectures; he didn't personally know of the injustices the agents mentioned—he thought his hamlet chief was all right, his grandfather owned several acres of land, and he had never heard a word about any elections—but he had no way of determining whether the injustices existed elsewhere, and the agents were so persuasive that he believed them. Kim was most eager for reunification. Many of his cousins, Viet Minh who had fought against the French, had gone north with their units in 1954, and he and their families missed them. If the country were whole again, they might return. The fact that two of Kim's older brothers had been killed by the Viet Minh while serving in the French Army left him with no ill feelings toward the Viet Minh. French troops had come to Binh Thuan on operations and had done a great deal of raping and stealing in the village. He thought his brothers would never have joined the French Army if they had seen French soldiers burn down their own parents' home, as Kim had. According to Kim, fear also played a part in his decision to join the Viet Cong. "I wasn't forced to join," he says, "but I felt a veiled threat, because the government seemed pretty indifferent or helpless to prevent the armed agents from coming into my village and taking people away for indoctrination." Kim also joined because he had no appealing alternative. He was the ninth of eleven children. Three of his brothers and sisters died of illness, in addition to the two brothers killed by the Viet Minh; Kim, two older sisters, one older brother, and two younger brothers survived. There was no primary school in Kim's hamlet. He started primary school in another hamlet in Binh Thuan village when he was twelve. He enjoyed school very much (mathematics was the subject he liked most, dictation the subject he liked least), but the road to school was flooded most of the time, making attendance difficult, and he gave up school after four years, and went to work in his grandfather's rice fields. He didn't care for the work. The V C also promised Kim he could stay near his village if he joined them, and he believed that if he was drafted into the government Army, he would be sent far from home. Kim had married a girl from another hamlet in Binh Thuan when he was eighteen. He had seen her at school and at the village market. Kim's father, a schoolteacher, had deserted the family when Kim was fourteen and had gone to live in another hamlet in the village with his mistress; Kim asked his mother to get the girl for him and she did. They had been happy together during the first three years of their marriage and had one son. Kim wanted to remain near his wife.

The day after Kim announced his decision, the agents took him to another nearby jungle base, which consisted of several well-concealed thatched huts on the bank of a creek. About thirty people, all of them South Vietnamese, lived there—ten armed senior agents and twenty newly recruited junior agents, who were not given arms. From the day they arrived at the base, Kim and the other new junior agents followed the same rigorous daily schedule—seven and a half hours of political studies, an hour and a half of physical exercise, and an hour of social life, which was devoted to learning revolutionary poems and songs. They were fed three skimpy meals a day, of rice and fish, or just rice and salt. At the political lectures, the senior agents dwelt on the evils of the Saigon government. The government was blamed over and over again for countless injustices, and for the **partition**[1] of the country. The lectures were followed by discussions of the ideas that had just been repeated for hours. "During the first month, I only listened to the lecturers," Kim says. "I didn't take part in the discussions. Then I got more interested, and I also realized that it didn't pay to keep silent, so I decided to be more talkative and to show more enthusiasm. I got through the initial period of political studies in two months. For those who didn't seem as receptive to the ideas as I was, political studies lasted as long as five

[1] **partition**—division.

or six months." The lecturers told Kim, a nominal Buddhist,[2] not to believe in the Buddha.

In March, 1958, Kim was given two hand grenades. He was assigned to escort senior agents on their nightly recruiting excursions to the villages in the area. He was supposed to help protect them and to master their recruiting technique. He still attended political lectures, but only for an hour or two a day. In November, 1959, as a result of having effectively escorted the senior agents and of having done well in his political training, he was made a cadre and became a senior recruiting agent. He was proud to be promoted. In early 1960, Kim was told of the imminent formation of a nationwide Liberation Front. He was also told that the revolutionary movement would soon become more **militant**.[3] He continued his nightly recruiting missions and his daily political studies and he was also given a little military training: he was taught how to fire, dismantle, and reassemble an old French bolt-action rifle. In his first two years with the VC, Kim saw his family only infrequently, at night, when he was on his way to a recruiting mission near his home. He was too busy in the daytime, studying or sleeping, and visits home were discouraged by his superiors. Although the food was bad and Kim had to ask his family for clothes and spending money (the VC weren't paid and were taught to regard the government soldiers as mercenaries) he was happy with his work.

On December 1, 1960, the sixty people at the base, some of them young men Kim had recruited, were divided into two groups. Thirty, including Kim, were assigned to the military section, thirty, to the political section. They were carefully primed by the senior agents for a night attack on Binh Thuan that was to take place

---

[2] Buddhist—one who follows the doctrine, attributed to Buddha, that suffering is inseparable from existence but that inward extinction of the self and of worldly desire culminates in a state of spiritual enlightenment beyond both suffering and existence.

[3] **militant**—combative or aggressive.

in mid-December. On the appointed night, both sections went together to Kim's native village. The political section had a few weapons, but their main duty was to shout slogans and declarations, urging people to rise up against the government. The military team's duty was to kill certain pre-selected government officials and supporters in the village. The VC took the village completely by surprise. They had several guns, but they didn't fire a shot. They used **scimitars**[4] to behead ten people in the seven hamlets in the village, including the chief of Kim's hamlet. Kim didn't kill his hamlet chief, but he killed five of the other victims, three men and two women. "It was the first time I'd done any killing, but it didn't upset me," he says. "Before we decided to kill those people, we discussed their misdeeds at length, and we had official documents to prove their guilt. The women were spies. I personally found out that they had hung up torches to warn government troops of our presence in the village when we came to recruit." That night, the government troops fired at the VC from a nearby outpost. They didn't hit any of them. After the attack, the VC returned to their jungle base.

Over the next year, Kim went on recruiting expeditions and also accompanied some of his comrades to villages in the area to **assassinate**[5] government officials and soldiers, and to capture badly needed weapons. At that time, the VC at the base were poorly armed, but in most villages there was only one **platoon**[6] of government militia, which couldn't protect an entire village. Government troops in nearby outposts became reluctant to leave their forts after they had been ambushed a few times when they had set out to rescue a hamlet.

---

[4] **scimitars**—curved Asian swords with the edge on the convex side.

[5] **assassinate**—to murder (a prominent person) by surprise attack, as for political reasons.

[6] **platoon**—a subdivision of a company of troops consisting of two or more sections and usually commanded by a lieutenant.

Occasionally, the VC clashed with government soldiers out on patrol. In one **skirmish**,[7] two Viet Cong were killed and Kim was wounded; a rifle bullet grazed his right knee. He was able to run about half a mile, and then had to be carried the rest of the way back to the base by his comrades. It took his wound two weeks to heal. In 1961, fifteen VC were killed; their losses were more than made up for by new recruits from the terrorized villages. That year, the VC at Kim's base killed about fifteen government officials and soldiers, and captured a number of guns. At the end of 1961, Kim was made a political cadre and was assigned to work with the youth in Binh Thuan. He gave them political education (while continuing his own political studies) and **incited**[8] them to destroy bridges, tear up roads, and demonstrate against the government.

In January, 1963, Kim was sent to a VC district headquarters near Binh Thuan. He stayed there a while and it was decided that he would be promoted from village guerrilla to the main force Viet Cong, on the basis of his good record. Kim was unhappy with this promotion. In the last five years, he had been able to spend very little time with his family, although he had never lived far from his hamlet. In 1962, his wife had left him and had returned to her father's home. Their son was living with Kim's mother. Kim wanted to be near his village, as he'd been promised when he joined the VC, so that he could see his child, but he was afraid to protest. He was sent to join a main force unit in Tay Ninh, another province in the **delta**.[9] It took Kim nearly two months to make the trip from Binh Thuan to a jungle camp a short distance from the provincial capital of Tay Ninh, a distance of only seventy-five miles. He and his companions walked

---

[7] **skirmish**—a minor battle in war, as one between small forces.

[8] **incited**—provoked or urged on.

[9] **delta**—a deposit of earth and sand that often occurs at the mouth of a river.

at night and had to check with local Viet Cong officials every step of the way. He reached his destination in early May, and was granted a week's rest. For the next six months, he was given his first real military training. He was taught to handle recoilless and automatic rifles, machine and submachine guns, carbines,[10] and mortars.[11] Kim was allowed to fire only one round of ammunition during his whole training period. He was told to shoot at a mark on the side of a deserted government outpost, from a distance of two hundred yards. He came close to the target and was considered a good marksman. The second time he fired was in actual combat. During his military training period, Kim spent an hour and a half a day on political studies. "In the late fifties, we were taught to fight against the national government, but after 1961, the one point driven home to us more than any other was the need to drive the American imperialists out of South Viet Nam," he says. "We were told to attack them at every opportunity, to keep them from taking over our country." In October, 1963, Kim was assigned to a main force battalion stationed in Tay Ninh province. He became a mortar crewman and had his first chance to fire the mortar on the night of November 1, 1963, when his battalion attacked a government outpost in a nearby province. Over the following months, Kim's battalion attacked a number of other government outposts, most of them in Tay Ninh province, and got into several minor and two major clashes with government troops. In February, 1964, when Kim's battalion was attacking an outpost in Tay Ninh, ten of his comrades were killed. Kim and four other VC were wounded. A bullet grazed Kim's thigh, but it didn't hit a bone and he required no surgery. The Viet Cong considered this a major engagement and a victory, because they

---

[10] carbines—lightweight rifles with short barrels.

[11] mortars—portable, muzzle-loading cannons used to fire shells at low velocities, short ranges, and high trajectories.

overran the outpost. In the second major clash, in July, 1964—the biggest action Kim has ever taken part in—his battalion attacked another outpost in Tay Ninh and ambushed a government relief column. The fighting went on **sporadically**[12] for two days and two nights. One hundred V C were killed and fifty wounded. Fifty government troops were killed and the battle was considered a defeat. "Practically all of our casualties were inflicted by bombers and armored personnel carriers," Kim says. "The airpower was so terrible we couldn't overrun the outpost and seize any weapons. With airpower, the V C could give the Army a much rougher time."

When they weren't fighting, Kim and the men in his battalion spent their time attending political lectures, receiving additional military training, and collecting provisions from the villages in the area. They sometimes slept at battalion headquarters, sometimes in V C villages, and sometimes, when traveling, in the jungle in hammocks. "It was especially uncomfortable when it was raining," Kim says. "We often had to work too hard when we were badly fed. But I liked the spirit of democracy and that made up for many things. We were free to criticize any officials or commanders, no matter how important they were, and they had to admit their shortcomings and promise to do better in the future. We didn't have to fear criticizing people. We were criticized often ourselves. Criticism sessions were held once a week."

At the end of August, 1964, Kim's mother came to Tay Ninh to see him. She begged him to leave the Viet Cong. Kim's older brother and one of his younger brothers were still in Binh Thuan, working in the rice fields, but one of his younger brothers had gone to Saigon to study and had become a government policeman. Kim's

---

[12] **sporadically**—intermittently; stopping and starting again.

mother was in tears when she told Kim she wanted her sons on one side. "I'd been having serious doubts about the V C and I wanted very much to be stationed back home again, but if my mother hadn't come to see me, I would have kept my rebellious ideas to myself," Kim says. "I felt very sorry when I saw my mother weeping. I began saying I wanted to go home, and I was severely criticized at the criticism sessions for being selfish. One day, I lost my temper. I almost shot a man who had criticized me especially sharply. As a result, I was sent to a reeducation center for **recalcitrant**[13] elements, in September, 1964." At the V C reeducation center in Tay Ninh province, Kim and forty other "recalcitrant elements" spent their time listening to political lectures and doing a few other chores, such as growing vegetables and building huts. They didn't have to fight. "During the first months, I couldn't help showing my resentment," Kim says. "I realized that wasn't getting me anywhere, so after a while I began to pose as a docile element and to master the lectures. After a few months, I was asked whether I wanted to continue with the Front or rejoin my family. I knew this was a test. No one is allowed to retire from the V C until he's very old, very sick, or seriously disabled. I was afraid to arouse suspicion, so I said I wanted to continue. They sent me out on several food-buying missions. I didn't try to escape, because I knew I was being watched closely. I was released from the reeducation center in July, 1965, and sent to a different regiment in Tay Ninh, to wait for a new assignment. The regiment was based in the jungle, very close to the Cambodian border." While waiting, Kim was sent out on various missions. Once, he was sent to a village about five miles from the regimental

---

[13] **recalcitrant**—stubbornly resistant.

base to tell the village cadres to take special care to prevent **defections**,[14] because the government was going to drop leaflets over the village describing its "Open Arms" program in the next few days. According to the government, Viet Cong who surrendered would receive **amnesty**[15] under the Open Arms program. The cadres were told to tell the VC that the program was a hoax, and that the government would torture defectors to death. Kim's regimental headquarters had received word of the imminent leaflet drop from VC infiltrated into the Open Arms program. Kim was often dispatched on food-buying missions. One day in August, 1965, he and three comrades were sent to a village a few miles from regimental headquarters to buy rice and fish. Dried fish was not available in the large quantity they had been ordered to get. Kim's friends returned to regimental headquarters in the afternoon, with the provisions they had succeeded in purchasing. Kim stayed on in the village to try to buy more fish. He spent the night under the watchful eyes of the local VC agents. The following day, there was a government operation in the village. The local VC cadres had to flee, so the tight VC control system was temporarily relaxed. Kim had been looking for an opportunity to defect from the Viet Cong. He decided that this was an excellent moment, because no one was watching him. He went to a farming area at the foot of the Black Lady mountain, where peasants were working in the rice fields under the protection of a government outpost. He stayed with the peasants until four in the afternoon, and then boarded a civilian bus with them. The bus took him to the provincial capital of Tay Ninh. When he arrived there, he asked his way to a police

---

[14] **defections**—acts of abandoning a position or an association, often to join an opposing group.

[15] **amnesty**—a general pardon granted by a government, especially for political offenses.

station. At the Tay Ninh police station, Kim told officials he had been a VC for seven and a half years, and had decided to defect to the government side. He asked for amnesty under the Open Arms program.

Kim had wanted to leave the Viet Cong ever since his transfer to the main forces in early 1963. He was tired of fighting. He had killed over fifteen people in addition to those he had killed in his village in December, 1960. He feared that he would be killed himself in the stepped-up fighting. He had also become disillusioned with the VC. "I was enthusiastic about the Viet Cong during my first years," Kim says. "I couldn't continue school, or do anything else I wanted to do, and I didn't like working in the rice fields. The VC seemed to be the only good chance I had to advance. When I was recruited, I was told that we would win in two years, and that all the people would be happy and the country reunified. After 1962, the prospect of victory and reunification grew dimmer, because the government was reinforced with American weapons and men. I was most enthusiastic about the Viet Cong in 1962, before my wife left me, when we were doing well and victory seemed to be in sight. Then I began to realize we might have to fight for years to reach the target we had thought within our easy reach. By early 1965, I even thought we might lose, if the Americans stuck it out in Viet Nam. We were told the Americans wouldn't stick it out, but we had been told in 1964 that the Americans wouldn't dare bomb North Viet Nam, and we knew that they eventually did. We also learned that the higher VC casualty figures were being hidden from us. It's true that our political education was intensive, but only fresh recruits believed entirely in what they were told. That's why most of the Front's real achievements are made by the young. People who have been with the

Front for some time have had opportunities to test their side's assets. They come to realize that a good deal of what the political **commissars**[16] taught was questionable. Many men who have been with the Front for a long time become dissatisfied and want to return to their families, but they don't act on their dissatisfaction. They are afraid, and they realize that once they've been in the Viet Cong, they don't have much of a future out of it. Many VC officials are really dedicated. They control the others, and push them to get things done. I probably would never have gotten started on the road to defection if my mother hadn't come to see me in Tay Ninh. I didn't like to see her weeping."

---

[16] **commissars**—officials of the Communist party in charge of political indoctrination and enforcement of party loyalty.

QUESTIONS TO CONSIDER

1. Who were the Viet Cong?

2. Why did Huynh Van Kim decide to join the Viet Cong?

3. Why did Kim's mother want him to leave the VC?

4. What caused Kim to become disillusioned with the VC?

Political Conflict

BY DON MOSER

Life in the villages of Vietnam was extremely difficult. For thirty years, soldiers of various nationalities fought for the land and the people's hearts: against the French, against the Viet Minh, against the Japanese, against the Viet Cong, against the Americans, against the North Vietnamese. For the villagers who just wanted to lead a peaceful life, it was a nightmare. Leaders were killed, buildings and villages razed, sons conscripted to fight by both sides, and so on. It was a life of unending violence. These villagers who all sides claimed to be fighting for were the real victims of the war. The following selection is from an article by Don Moser, a reporter for Life *magazine who covered the war from 1966–69, describing life in a South Vietnamese village.*

LOC DIEN, VIETNAM. Early on Monday morning, while the haze still blurs the dark bulk of Truoi Mountain off to the east, the old men walk through the village of Loc Dien. Like a line of ravens in their black formal robes, and holding their black umbrellas, they walk slowly, almost in lock step, through the pale green fields of young rice toward the house of the father of the vice chief. Behind them trudges Ngo Truy, the village policeman, looking out of place in his khakis and white sun helmet, and carrying his carbine over his shoulder. Truy is burly for a Vietnamese, but with large, dark eyes and a gentle manner that seems **incongruous**[1] for a cop. He looks tired and he is, for he has been awake ever since he heard the shots at midnight. At first light he found the two bodies on a jungle path: one, the father of the vice chief; the other, a Buddhist leader. Pinned to their chests were statements accusing them of using their influence to turn the villagers against the National Liberation Front—the Vietcong. The V.C. had shot the vice chief's father through the chest, and treated the Buddhist leader with **sacrilegious**[2] contempt—the whole front of his head was crushed in, and between his eyes was a bullet hole you could stick your thumb in. The head is very sacred to the Buddhists.

The delegation of old men finally reaches a clearing around the house of the father of the vice chief. It is a neat building of cement painted sky blue. Inside are a few wooden tables and benches where other old men sit, looking very formal and **sage**[3] in their black robes as they sip pale tea. As Truy and the visitors enter, Chuong, the vice chief, comes out from behind a curtain at the back of the room. Chuong is not a pretty man—one of his eyes has a wandering cast—and now his face is drawn with grief, but he politely greets Truy and the others, offers them tea, and draws back the curtains.

The body of the old man, his father, lies on a wooden bed. It is wrapped in a sheet and the face is covered by a piece of paper. To the right, incense smolders; to the left, an oil lamp burns. The old men in black move forward to look.

---

[1] **incongruous**—incompatible.

[2] **sacrilegious**—grossly irreverent toward what is or is held to be sacred.

[3] **sage**—wise.

As they do, someone from outside begins to scream. Chuong's sister, who lives in a nearby hamlet, has heard the news. Now she bursts out of the jungle, running, her mouth wide open as she shrieks, the noise rising in pitch and volume. Dashing across the clearing she stumbles, then comes on staggering, tearing off her **conical**[4] hat and flinging it aside. She lurches through the door to throw herself on the body on the bed.

"Cha oi, cha di mo? Cha di mo?" she moans. "My father, where have you gone?" As she clutches at the body, the sheet slips aside, exposing one of the old man's hands. It is the hand of a farmer, brown, with dirt under the cracked nails, strong-looking even in death.

"Why have you left me?" the girl screams harshly. "You were innocent. Why did the Vietcong kill you?"

The country village of Loc Dien lies some 400 miles north of Saigon, near the old Imperial capital of Hue. Ten thousand people live in Loc Dien. The village consists of 13 hamlets or neighborhoods, sprawling for six kilometers along the River Truoi. Loc Dien lies in lush, tropical country, and its little hamlets are tucked away among thickets of bamboo and trees that hang with bananas, coconuts and breadfruit bigger than a man's head. Loc Dien is prosperous by Vietnamese standards, and lovely by any standard. Along with the peasant huts of **lath**[5] and buffalo dung are many houses made of cement, again painted a distinctive blue; here and there throughout the village are little one-room elementary schools, and an occasional small Buddhist pagoda. Most peasants have some land of their own, and around the houses the jungle is checkered with small fields of rice, tea, corn, potatoes, and garden truck. On Loc Dien's few dusty streets, and on the jungle trails that connect the hamlets, pretty schoolgirls ride their bicycles, the long

---

[4] **conical**—shaped like a cone.

[5] **lath**—a thin strip of wood or metal, usually nailed in rows to framing supports as a substructure.

skirts of their white ao dais flowing gracefully behind. In the hamlet by the Bay of the Two Bridges small boys wade in the waist-deep water, beating rhythmically with bamboo poles as they drive tiny fish into the nets held by their parents. The farmers plow their fields behind hump-shouldered water buffalo, or sit for hours pedaling crude pumps which lift water from the irrigation ditches up over small dikes into the rice paddies. The wives heap their produce, in top-heavy piles that defy gravity, on the tops of rattletrap buses that run to the big markets in Hue; or they carry their goods in baskets to the market in the village, where they squat all day, amicably chatting among themselves and chewing cuds of mildly narcotic betel nut.[6]

But Loc Dien is not so tranquil as it seems. Beneath the peaceful surface, the struggle between the government and the Vietcong goes on night and day. By day most of the village belongs to the government. But the night is a different matter. Eight times this year alone, small bands of Vietcong have come down from Truoi Mountain after dark, dragged a villager from his bed and shot him dead. Scores of other villagers have been kidnapped and taken away into the forest for political "education." The highway that bisects the village has been mined. Grenades have been thrown into the market place. Almost every day people find leaflets which the Vietcong have strewn the night before. Or they hear rumors from woodcutters who have encountered Vietcong in the jungle. Both leaflets and rumors promise future violence. Not long ago the Vietcong left a leaflet that named eight influential villagers they promised to execute. . . . For these men, and for the villagers as a whole, fear is something one gets up with in the morning and goes to bed with at night.

---

[6] betel nut—the seed of the betel palm, chewed with betel leaves, lime, and flavorings as a mild stimulant.

The hub of the village of Loc Dien is the great steel bridge on which Highway One and the Vietnam Railway—the only lines of ground transportation between Hue, to the north, and the American military stronghold of Da Nang, to the south—cross the slow-rolling River Truoi. Just to the north of the bridge is the barbed-wire enclosure of an old French fort which now serves as the garrison for a Vietnamese army battalion. Just south of the bridge, in Loc Dien proper, is the railroad station, a small dispensary, and a cluster of metal-roofed open-front shops. Off the highway, on Loc Dien's dirt main street, is the village office. And there, on the Monday morning following the two assassinations, the chief of the village works at his battered desk. In the evening Nguyen Dong likes to go about barefoot and clad in floppy trousers and an undershirt, but now he wears sandals and a shirt neatly pressed in accordance with his high station. A limp, home-rolled cigarette dangles from his lower lip, dribbling ash on his papers as he works.

At 55, Dong is, in effect, the mayor of Loc Dien. He is a civilian. The chiefs of Vietnam's larger political units—the districts (equivalent to our counties) and provinces (equivalent to our states)—are army officers, military governors with enormous authority. Dong must answer to his district chief whose headquarters are 14 kilometers to the south, but Loc Dien itself, like all Vietnamese villages, is a little democracy. The chief, his vice chief, and the chiefs of the 13 hamlets are elected every other year by all the adults of the village. With his small staff—a policeman, a tax collector, an information officer, and a few clerks—Dong worries about everything from issuing marriage licenses to protecting his people from the V.C.

Nguyen Dong is tired. He has had a lifetime of war and public service. Between his inheritance from his father, a prosperous farmer, and the **canny**[7] investment of his own salary in land, Dong has acquired two good cement-block houses, four water buffalo and six hectares (about 15 acres) of rice land. But he must find someone else to work his rice fields, since he dares not work in such an exposed situation himself. He has not slept in either of his fine houses for more than two years. Dong's name heads the Vietcong assassination list and he must steep each night on a cot in the railway station, where all the hamlet chiefs and village officials gather. There a handful of village soldiers can guard them all. Sometimes Dong wishes he could quit his job as chief, but in the last election 90% of the villagers voted for him, and now he cannot resign. "I would lose their respect," he says simply.

Dong can hardly remember a time of serenity in Loc Dien. When he was a young man, the country was run by the French, through a puppet emperor. Late in World War II came the Japanese, harsh and unpredictable, and then Ho Chi Minh's Communist Vietminh. In 1947 the French began their attempt to push the Vietminh out of the Loc Dien area and there followed seven years of being in the middle of a guerrilla war. It was not very much different from today, with the villagers fearing and despising the French and Vietminh almost equally. Then, too, there were assassinations, night raids and reprisals. Dong's father was kidnapped by the Vietminh one night and never seen again. Six months after that, the Vietminh returned and burned Dong's house to the ground.

For a while, after the country was partitioned in 1954, the village had a taste of peace and growing prosperity. But by the late '50s, President Diem—and his detested brother and sister-in-law, the Nhus—had lost touch with the countryside. The Communists, who called themselves

---

[7] **canny**—careful and shrewd, especially where one's own interests are concerned.

the National Liberation Front, became active again. The succession of coups and governmental overthrows since Diem's death have bewildered Dong and his villagers. They wonder cynically whether the Saigon government will ever be stabilized. Meanwhile, the amount of Vietcong influence in the village has grown steadily.

Dong maintains that only 5% of the villagers sympathize with the Vietcong. Only a few young men have gone off to the mountain to join them. But at night Loc Dien is so insecure that people tremble with fear every time a dog barks. Recently the Vietcong have attempted to drop mortar shells onto the Vietnamese battalion garrisoned at the old French fort—something they could do only by setting up their weapons within the borders of the village. But some of the rounds have been short and the villagers who live near the fort have had to dig fox holes and tunnels beneath their houses. On the 80-kilometer stretch between Hue and Da Nang the V.C. blow or mine the road and railway every night, so that rice and other goods imported from the south have almost doubled in price over the last few months. Now people can hardly afford to buy the food they need. The railroad-highway bridge over the River Truoi, just 50 yards from Dong's office, is a prime military target, and in the propaganda leaflets left by tile V.C. they have promised to attack it. They have also promised to attack the railway station where Dong and the others sleep at night. They have promised to get an old friend of Dong's named Hach and cut him in half. And just yesterday the boy who herds Dong's water buffalo heard a rumor that the V.C. plan to throw a grenade into Dong's house to kill his wife and his children.

Dong rarely sees an American, for none is stationed in the village. But once in a while, when the battalion garrisoned across the river is home from the field, its American and Australian advisers come to Loc Dien for a glass of beer, or an American medic holds sick call for the villagers. When the Americans first came, the people feared they would be like the French. But the Americans played with the children, who soon followed them in droves, shouting "Hello, OK," and they were off-handedly friendly to everyone, not offending the villagers' pride, as did the French, by treating them like inferior beings. Now, when the V.C. leaflets say that the Americans rob the people of food and leave the hamlets with their pockets bulging with stolen bananas, Dong and the villagers laugh. . . .

That evening Bui Van Cach, the young chief of Su Lo Dong hamlet, loads a round into the chamber of his carbine, hooks a couple of fragmentation grenades to his belt, says goodnight to his wife and children and goes out into the jungle. Cach is No. 6 on the V.C. assassination list—for the best of reasons. He likes to fight. A handsome, dynamic fellow of 33, he was in a Vietnamese commando outfit that fought against the Vietminh, and since returning to civilian life he has lost none of his aggressiveness. Come nightfall, when the other 12 hamlet chiefs sleep in the comparatively secure railroad station, Cach and an odd little band of warriors lie in ambush for the Vietcong.

At dusk they assemble—as motley a group of irregular soldiers as can be imagined. Nine of the men are peasants, wearing shorts and sandals and conical peasant hats. And Nguyen Che, who in the daytime is custodian of the village elementary schools, has completed his nightly metamorphosis into a squad leader. Festooned with grenades and flares that he has scrounged from friends in the army, with a carbine in one hand, a swagger stick in the other and a cocked .45 in his belt, he cuts a figure that is simultaneously fearsome and absurd. But the Vietcong find nothing funny about him, and they have spread the word that for the death of Nguyen Che, or for any of the men in his squad, they will pay a bounty of 5,000 piasters.[8]

Bui Van Cach is intensely proud of his little group. "The V.C. are afraid to come here," he says with a grin all across his round brown face. "The people in this hamlet believe this hamlet will never be attacked. The people say we are their men, not government men. They do not have to be afraid when dogs bark at night."

Now, in the gathering dusk, Cach and the grenade-laden Che move through the hamlet, informing trusted peasants where they will spend the night in case there is any trouble. Then, with their squad, they set out trip flares along the jungle trails to tip them off to any V.C. movements, and disappear into a patch of jungle near the hamlet border to lie in wait for whatever may come.

Later this same Friday night, as Cach and his men wait in the jungle, policeman Truy is also awake, standing beneath the banana trees near the railroad station and peering out into the darkness. Truy and his Popular Forces squad also lay ambushes for the V.C., but they have the additional responsibility of guarding the officials who sleep in the railroad station. So Truy never has enough men available to pose a serious problem for the V.C.

At midnight, after checking on his guards, Truy goes on into the railway station and stretches out on a mat on the concrete floor, his arm for a pillow. An hour and a half later he is shaken awake. One of the men from the patrol tells him excitedly that they have just spotted a strong V.C. unit moving up the highway toward the railroad station. Quickly Truy wakes the sleeping men. His nine soldiers and all the hamlet chiefs who possess weapons are posted at windows and among the trees just outside the station. He has 17 guns in all, and hopes it will be enough. The battalion

---

[8] piasters—a unit of currency in former South Vietnam.

from the fort across the river is away on an operation and Truy knows he can expect no help. If only he had a B.A.R.,[9] it would make a difference.

At 2 o'clock the night is shattered by the fire of automatic weapons as the V.C. attack suddenly from three sides. Bullets spit and whine off the concrete facing of the building. Truy grabs his carbine and starts firing rapidly at the points of muzzle flashes out in the darkness. Screaming, "We will cut off your heads!" the V.C. press forward three times and try to throw grenades through the windows, but each time the grenades fall short. Then Nguyen Lach, one of Truy's soldiers, falls to the ground, his skull creased by a ricochet. A few minutes later, by the light of a flare, Truy sees the Vietcong dragging a wounded comrade away and the attack ends as abruptly as it began.

Next night, the V.C. attack again. Once more they try to grenade the railway station; once more Truy and his men beat them off. But this time the attack is just a diversion. Half an hour later another band of V.C. attacks a highway bridge near the school where Cao held his meeting. But they, too, are driven off by the bridge guards.

---

[9] B.A.R.—Browning automatic rifle.

QUESTIONS TO CONSIDER

1. Do the Loc Dien villagers like Americans? Why or why not?

2. How do the people of Loc Dien feel about the war?

3. How are Bui Van Cach and his band of soldiers different from the "government men"?

War for a Viet Cong

BY TRUONG NHU TANG

*Truong Nhu Tang was a French-educated lawyer, who while living
and working in South Vietnam, devoted himself to the cause of
the Viet Cong. After the Communist victory, Tang was horrified by
the repression of the new regime and left Vietnam for France.
A Viet Cong Memoir (1985) is Tang's account of his fight against
the Americans. In the following excerpt, Tang describes what it
was like to be caught in a U.S. bombardment. Between 1965 and
1973, U.S. planes flew 526,000 sorties in Vietnam and dropped
more than 6 million tons of explosives on the country. It is an
extraordinary number when you consider that it is three times the
number of bombs dropped by all of the countries fighting during
World War II.*

Infiltrating into areas under secure government control to see wives and children who had often been
marked as Vietcong dependents was a chance business.
To get around this, from time to time we would be able
to bring families out to the jungle, something that was

done for soldiers as well as **cadres.**[1] But such meetings were necessarily brief and dangerous themselves. (Vo Van Kiet's wife and children were killed on their way to one such rendezvous, when they were caught in a B-52[2] raid.) More often than not these men went for extended periods without any contact at all with their families.

But for all the **privations**[3] and hardships, nothing the guerrillas had to endure compared with the stark terrorization of the B-52 bombardments. During its involvement, the United States dropped on Vietnam more than three times the tonnage of explosives that were dropped during all of World War II in military theaters that spanned the world. Much of it came from the high altitude B-52s, bombs of all sizes and types being disgorged by these invisible predators. The statistics convey some sense of the concentrated firepower that was unleashed at America's enemies in both North and South. From the perspective of those enemies, these figures translated into an experience of undiluted psychological terror, into which we were plunged, day in, day out for years on end.

From a kilometer away, the sonic roar of the B-52 explosions tore eardrums, leaving many of the jungle dwellers permanently deaf. From a kilometer, the shock waves knocked their victims senseless. Any hit within a half kilometer would collapse the walls of an unreinforced bunker, burying alive the people cowering inside. Seen up close, the bomb craters were gigantic— thirty feet across and nearly as deep. In the rainy seasons they would fill up with water and often saw service as duck or fishponds, playing their role in the

---

[1] **cadres**—trained personnel.

[2] **B-52**—the Boeing B-52 was a long-distance U.S. bomber, first built in the 1950s. The B-52G version, which was developed in 1958, was able to carry nuclear weapons to any global target at short notice.

[3] **privation**—lack of the basic necessities or comforts of life.

guerrillas' never-ending quest to broaden their diet. But they were treacherous then too. For as the swamps and lowland areas flooded under half a foot of standing water, the craters would become invisible. Not infrequently some surprised guerrilla, wading along what he had taken to be a familiar route, was suddenly swallowed up.

It was something of a miracle that from 1968 through 1970 the attacks, though they caused significant casualties generally, did not kill a single one of the military or civilian leaders in the headquarters complexes. This luck, though, had a lot to do with accurate advance warning of the raids, which allowed us to move out of the way or take refuge in our bunkers before the bombs began to rain down. B-52s flying out of Okinawa and Guam would be picked up by Soviet intelligence trawlers plying the South China Sea. The planes' headings and air speed would be computed and relayed to COSVN[4] headquarters, which would then order NLF[5] or Northern elements in the anticipated target zones to move away perpendicularly to the attack trajectory. Flights originating from the Thai bases were monitored both on radar and visually by our intelligence nets there and the information similarly relayed.

Often the warnings would give us time to grab some rice and escape by foot or bike down one of the emergency routes. Hours later we would return to find, as happened on several occasions, that there was nothing left. It was as if an enormous scythe had swept through the jungle, felling the giant teak and go trees like grass in its way, shredding them into billions of scattered splinters. On these occasions—when the B-52s had found

---

[4] COSVN—reference to Communist headquarters in South Vietnam.
[5] NLF—National Liberation Front.

their mark—the complex would be utterly destroyed: food, clothes, supplies, documents, everything. It was not just that things were destroyed; in some awesome way they had ceased to exist. You would come back to where your lean-to and bunker had been, your home, and there would simply be nothing there, just an unrecognizable landscape gouged by immense craters.

Equally often, however, we were not so fortunate and had time only to take cover as best we could. The first few times I experienced a B-52 attack it seemed, as I strained to press myself into the bunker floor, that I had been caught in the Apocalypse.[6] The terror was complete. One lost control of bodily functions as the mind screamed incomprehensible orders to get out. On one occasion a Soviet delegation was visiting our ministry when a particularly short-notice warning came through. When it was over, no one had been hurt, but the entire delegation had sustained considerable damage to its dignity—uncontrollable trembling and wet pants the all-too-obvious outward signs of inner convulsions. The visitors could have spared themselves their feelings of embarrassment; each of their hosts was a veteran of the same symptoms.

It was a tribute to the Soviet surveillance techniques that we were caught aboveground so infrequently during the years of the deluge. One of these occasions, though, almost put an end to all our endeavors. Taken by surprise by the sudden earthshaking shocks, I began running along a trench toward my bunker opening when a huge concussion lifted me off the ground and propelled me through the doorway toward which I was heading. Some of my Alliance colleagues were knocked off their feet and rolled around the ground like rag dolls. One old friend, Truong Cao Phuoc, who

---

[6] Apocalypse—the end of the world, as prophesied in the Bible.

was working in the foreign relations division, had jumped into a shelter that collapsed on him, somehow leaving him alive with his head protruding from the ground. We extricated him, shoveling the dirt out handful by handful, carefully removing the supporting timbers that were crisscrossed in the earth around him. Truong had been trapped in one of the old U-shaped shelters, which became graves for so many. Later we learned to reinforce these dugouts with an A-frame of timbers that kept the walls from falling in. Reinforced in this manner, they could withstand B-52 bomb blasts as close as a hundred meters.

Sooner or later, though, the shock of the bombardments wore off, giving way to a sense of abject **fatalism.**[7] The veterans would no longer scrabble at the bunker floors convulsed with fear. Instead people just resigned themselves—fully prepared to "go and sit in the ancestors' corner." The B-52s somehow put life in order. Many of those who survived the attacks found that afterward they were capable of viewing life from a more serene and philosophical perspective. It was a lesson that remained with me, as it did with many others, and helped me compose myself for death on more than one future occasion.

But even the most philosophical of fatalists were worn to the breaking point after several years of dodging and burrowing away from the rain of high explosives. During the most intense periods we came under attack every day for weeks running. At these times we would cook our rice as soon as we got out of our hammocks, kneading it into glutinous[8] balls and ducking into the bunkers to be ready for what we

---

[7] **fatalism**—the doctrine that all events are predetermined by fate and are therefore unalterable.

[8] glutinous—gummy; having the quality of glue.

knew was coming. Occasionally, we would be on the move for days at a time, stopping only to prepare food, eating as we walked. At night we would sling our hammocks between two trees wherever we found ourselves, collapsing into an exhausted but restless sleep, still half-awake to the inevitable explosions.

Pursued relentlessly by such demons, some of the guerrillas suffered nervous breakdowns and were packed off for hospital stays; others had to be sent home. There were cases too of fighters rallying to the Saigon government, unable to cope with the demands of life in the jungle. Times came when nobody was able to manage, and units would seek a hopeful refuge across the border in Cambodia.

QUESTIONS TO CONSIDER

1. Why were the B-52 raids so terrifying?

2. What lessons about life and death did the guerrillas learn from the B-52 attacks?

3. What surprised you about Truong Nhu Tang's recollections?

from

One Very Hot Day

BY DAVID HALBERSTAM

The war in Vietnam was ostensibly between South Vietnam and the Viet Cong. The South Vietnamese army (Army of the Republic of Vietnam or ARVN) was engaged in trying to put down the Viet Cong guerrillas. In reality, the U.S. and the North Vietnamese were the combatants. The North Vietnamese not only supported the Viet Cong but also, when it became apparent that the war would not be easily won, began sending units of the North Vietnamese army to fight in the South. The U.S. started as an advisor to the ARVN, but by 1965 was fighting a war against Communism. This led to obvious confusion about who was fighting whom and for what. It was particularly difficult for the ARVN who were treated as second-class soldiers by their American allies and as traitors by other Vietnamese. The journalist David Halberstam's novel One Very Hot Day *(1967) includes both U.S. and ARVN soldiers as characters. In the following excerpt from* One Very Hot Day, *an ARVN officer describes his war.*

There was a terrible quality of truth to what Thuong had just heard and he did not like it; he had not liked the operation from the start and he had always disagreed with Headquarters and Staff over the area. Staff called it a blue area (the Americans, he decided, loved maps even more than the French and had taught them about red, white and blue areas; the Americans loved to change the colors, to turn red into white and white into blue, to put red pins on white spots and blue pins on red spots) and blue was supposed to be secure, but Thuong had never liked the area; he did not operate there often and so he tended to accept the Headquarters' version of the area as being secure, only to find once they were in the area that it was not quite what it seemed, that it was always a little more hostile than the authorities claimed. He suspected that it was a Communist area where the guerrillas did little in the way of challenging the government and were content to rest somewhat tranquil on the surface, using it as a communications path. The Arvin[1] recruited, Thuong remembered, few government soldiers from the area, and the young men they did take showed a higher desertion rate than might have been expected.

He walked beside the suspect, near the rear of the column. "I believe you have told us the truth," he told the prisoner.

The man did not look up at him.

"Perhaps you will be free by the end of the day," Thuong said.

"Perhaps, we will all be dead by the end of the day," the prisoner said a little bitterly.

"Would you like some of my water?" Thuong asked.

The prisoner said no, but then asked if Thuong would do him a favor: "You believe me and know what I say is true." Thuong said yes, he would do the favor, if he could, depending on what it was.

"Would you tie my hands together?" the prisoner asked. "You see if they see me walking with you . . ."

---

[1] Arvin—ARVN, or Army of the Republic of Vietnam.

"I know," Thuong said, and ordered his hands bound; the Americans, he thought, should have asked this peasant whether he thought the area was blue or red. Perhaps they should explain that it was safe to walk free, that it was blue.

"You are not from here, are you?" the prisoner asked.

"No," said the Lieutenant, "I come from the north."

"I know, but you are not like the other northerners, you are nicer than them."

"Only because you are more honest than the other southerners," he said.

Thuong trusted the man although he did not trust southerners in general; he thought of them as dishonest, a little too lazy for their own good, a little too willing to tell you what you wanted to hear, always dependent on their women to do their work (almost, he thought, a pride in this, the best man was the one whose woman worked the hardest). He thought of northerners as being more honest, although the northerners who had come south like himself were no longer particularly honest; they had to bend enough themselves in order to survive.

Thuong was thirty-one, though, like most Vietnamese, he looked younger to foreign eyes. He was slim and his face seemed almost innocent; he had been in the Government Army too long to be innocent, eight years, and all of them either as **aspirant**[2] or lieutenant. His lack of advancement was no particular reflection on his ability, indeed, those few superiors who took the time to monitor his file, such as it was with more papers missing than enclosed, were surprised at the degree of achievement and ability; having achieved this surprise, however, they did not feel obligated to increase his rank or command. Indeed the older he got, and the more papers there were in praise of him—including, dangerously American praise—the more it tended to

---

[2] **aspirant**—one who aspires, as to advancement, honors, or a high position.

mitigate against him; here after all was a man of ability who had not gotten ahead. Therefore, there must be something wrong, something unseen but known, something political; his superiors were in particular surprised by his father's choice of religion. His father, having associated with foreigners in the north, did not choose to convert; he worked closely with foreigners and dutifully accepted their pay and their orders, but not their religion. This was unusual for the time; there were, after all, many Vietnamese who began to dress like the French, eat like the French, and talk like the French. His father referred to them all as the "mustache-Vietnamese" in honor of their copying French-style mustaches. Thuong had once gently asked his father about this, why he had never taken their faith, and his father had said simply that he was paid for his manual contributions, not his spiritual ones. Nevertheless, he was closely associated with foreigners and during the beginning of the French war, he had continued to work for them, as much by accident as by decision (he did not particularly like them, but he had a vague feeling that since everyone else was deserting the foreigners, it was improper for him to do it as well); one of his objections after all to the French had been the contempt they had showed toward Vietnamese people and their obvious belief that all Vietnamese were cowards, to leave now would be to confirm all the worst things the French had said. When the foreigners by their stupidity, which his father could not have been expected to have foreseen, lost the war, thereby proving to the French that all Vietnamese were not cowards and making his father's original reason somewhat obsolete, it was decided to split up the family and come to the south, splitting up into small groups so that they wouldn't be stopped by the local Vietminh bands.

The way had been difficult from the start and Thuong's grandmother, who was in his charge, had nearly died from exhaustion. (Later Thuong remembered trying to find water for her, giving her all his water, and the terrible thirst that had stayed with him for days at a time. When he thought of the division of the country, he thought of his own thirst.) When they finally arrived in the south, they turned out to be among the few Buddhists who had made the trip, and were immediately placed in a camp for Catholic refugees. There they shared the difficult position of the Catholics of being unwanted immigrants in the south, without sharing either their faith or their protection.

On the basis of his father's connections, he had managed to attend a military school, after first lingering on the waiting list for a year and a half. There he quickly discovered that he was a northerner in the south, a Buddhist among Catholics, and thus at almost any given time lacked the proper credentials. The southerners did not trust him because he was a northerner, the Catholics did not trust him because he was a Buddhist. In a country **shorn**[3] of **idealism**[4] and reeking of **cynicism**[5] and **opportunism,**[6] he was an object of suspicion. So he remained a lieutenant; as they remained suspicious of him, so he in turn became distrustful and cynical about them. He accepted the legacy of being his father's son with the same fatalism, largely because he could think of no real alternative to it and because if it offered nothing else, it offered him a certain sense of privacy and individualism. He went along with their rules but he tried to remain himself. He envied the Communists their self-belief, their **ideology,**[7] their

---

[3] **shorn**—deprived.

[4] **idealism**—the act or practice of envisioning things in an ideal form.

[5] **cynicism**—scornful quality or disposition.

[6] **opportunism**—taking advantage of any opportunity to achieve, often with no regard for principles or consequences.

[7] **ideology**—a set of doctrines or beliefs that form the basis of a political, economic, or other system.

certainty, even their cruelty; the Catholics, their convictions and connections; the Americans, their intensity and idealism; and his father, his gentleness and enduring innocence (his father, embarrassed and uneasy and unworldly, periodically would ask him if he *had* to be a soldier, wasn't there something else he could do; his father knew, of course, that it paid well . . .); he doubted what he did and he suspected that the war would probably be lost. It was not that he wished to be on the other side—that would be easy to do, a short walk away during an operation—nor that he thought the other side more just: the Communists, after all, had killed an uncle, just as the French had stupidly managed to kill a cousin, wiping out a village (until then pro-French) as the Vietminh had planned for them to do. The Vietminh side was as cruel as the French, and lacked only the corruption of the French. He suspected that ten years of power would improve their sense of corruption (depending, he thought, on the degree of success of their system; they would need a certain amount of success to be corrupt. If their system failed, they could retain their **integrity**[8]). The danger of going over, he thought, would not be that he had been fighting them all these years and had killed many of their people (they, unlike the Arvin, would have real records and they would know who he was, and who he had killed); nor that after the minimal comfort of My Tho, with its soda pop and iced beer, that life would be too rigorous. It was simply that he knew he was too cynical for the passion and commitment their life took. To gain religion in Vietnam, he thought, you must start very young; to retain it, he thought, you have to be very lucky. . . .

So he continued his own way: he did not desert because it would hurt his parents (and also because it

---

[8] **integrity**—steadfast adherence to a strict moral or ethical code.

would make no difference to him) and so his life had made him a very old lieutenant. The particular reward that he now enjoyed for his fatalism was Captain Dang. The Captain was a year younger than Thuong and had been in the army for a shorter time, and was soon to be a major, according to Dang himself. He was well connected in Saigon and was aware of this; he visited Saigon frequently, and he often referred to the dinners and parties he had just attended. He frequently praised Thuong (in front of Thuong, implying that he had also praised Thuong in those same great halls); he talked of promotion for Thuong, something, Thuong was virtually sure, if it ever came, would come in spite of Dang. Dang did not know the name of anyone in the unit below the rank of corporal; he cheated on the ranks, regularly turning in more men than he actually had, failing to report losses (the advantage being that he was not reprimanded for losing men, and at the same time continued to draw their pay. The result was that the company which should have been under-strength by ten men was usually understrength about two dozen, and the pressure on the men was even greater than it should have been). Thuong had compensated for this in part by commandeering an extra light machine gun from a friend in another company: the company had lost it, then captured it back in a long battle with the Vietcong battalion. Since it had already been reported lost, it was surplus on the rolls and Thuong had been owed a major favor by his friend—he had lent them three men during a key inspection. Thuong was careful to pay as little attention as possible to Dang's corruption; Dang, indeed, was convenient for Thuong. He fitted Thuong's own view of what an officer was, what the system was, and made his own lack of promotion easier to bear; it would have been more bitter were Dang a real soldier.

But for two years and a half now, he had despised Dang over one incident. It was a time just before the American helicopters had arrived with their remarkable ability to bring in reinforcement, and there was still a terrible isolation to battle: you were hit and you stayed there alone and fought it out. There had been an ambush, a brief and bitter one, and Thuong at first had been paralyzed like everyone else, sure that he was going to die there; but he had in those first minutes seen something he would never forgive and never forget (particularly since when he saw it, he expected it to be one of the last things he ever saw): Dang taking off his officer's pips.[9] If you are going to wear the pips in the great halls of Saigon, he thought, you must wear them in the U Minh forest.

---

[9] pips—shoulder insignias used to indicate the rank of certain officers.

QUESTIONS TO CONSIDER

1. What is Thuong's attitude toward the war?

2. What is the "dominant feature" of Thuong's personality?

3. Why does Thuong despise Dang?

A Civilian's Tale

BY LE LY HAYSLIP

*While the soldiers of all the armies in Vietnam certainly suffered,
it was the civilians who bore the worst parts of the war. The
villages of South Vietnam were endlessly fought over, and each side
committed terrible atrocities against the Vietnamese farmers.
Le Ly Hayslip (1949–) was born in the village of Ky La in central
Vietnam. In 1961, the war came to Ky La, and for the next nine
years Hayslip struggled to survive in an ever-changing world.
Members of her family were killed, beaten, coerced into fighting,
and imprisoned. She herself suffered rape, imprisonment, and
torture. In 1970, Hayslip married an American soldier and escaped
to the United States. Her memoir* When Heaven and Earth
Changed Places *is an eloquent statement of what happened to
the Vietnamese peasant who both sides claimed to be fighting for.
In the following excerpt, Hayslip, who is living in Da Nang with
most of her family, makes a dangerous journey back to Ky La to
check on her father.*

I left my mother at sunrise praying for my safety.
Both she and Ba had tried to discourage me from making the trip—saying there were rumors that my father
had been beaten and that danger was everywhere—but

they understood neither the risks I had already taken in my business nor the fact that I now knew Americans to be a bit less brutal and more trustworthy than either the Vietnamese or Viet Cong forces. To avoid combatants on either side, I traced the route I had taken in the storm almost three years before, through the swamps, jungle, hills, and brush country from Danang to Marble Mountain to Ky La but this time the weather was fine and I had plenty of time to think about my father and what to do when I got home. When I arrived, however, the village I remembered no longer existed.

Half of Ky La had been leveled to give the Americans a better "killing zone" when defending the village. Their camp, which was a complex of bunkers and trenches with tin roofs, sandbags, radio antennas, and tents, lorded over the village from a hilltop outside of town. Around its slopes, homeless peasants and little kids poked through the American garbage in hopes of finding food or something to sell. In the distance, through a screen of withered trees (which had been defoliated now by chemicals as well as bombs), I could see that Bat Gian had not been rebuilt, and that the few remaining temples, pagodas, and wayside shrines—even my old schoolhouse and the guardsmen's awful prison—had been wiped away by the hand of war. Beautiful tropical forests had been turned into a bomb-cratered desert. It was as if the American giant, who had for so long been taunted and annoyed by the Viet Cong ants, had finally come to stamp its feet—to drive the painted, smiling Buddha from his house and substitute instead the khaki, glowering God of Abraham.

With the sickening feeling that I was now a stranger in my own homeland, I crossed the last few yards to my house with a lump in my throat and a growing sense of dread. Houses could be rebuilt and damaged dikes repaired—but the loss of our temples and shrines meant the death of our culture itself. It meant that a generation of children would grow up without fathers to teach them about their ancestors or the rituals of worship. Families would lose records of their lineage and with them the umbilicals to the very root of our society—not just old buildings and books, but people who once lived and loved like them. Our ties to our past were being severed, setting us adrift on a sea of borrowed Western materialism, disrespect for the elderly, and selfishness. The war no longer seemed like a fight to see which view would prevail. Instead, it had become a fight to see just how much and how far the Vietnam of my ancestors would be transformed. It was as if I was standing by the cradle of a dying child and speculating with its aunts and uncles on what the doomed baby would have looked like had it grown up. By tugging on their baby so brutally, both parents had wound up killing it. Even worse, the war now attacked Mother Earth—the seedbed of us all. This, to me, was the highest crime—the frenzied suicide of cannibals. How shall one mourn a lifeless planet?

Inside, the neat, clean home of my childhood was a hovel. What few furnishings and tools were left after the battles had been looted or burned for fuel. Our household shrine, which always greeted new arrivals as the centerpiece of our family's pride, was in shambles. Immediately I saw the bag of bones and torn sinew that was my father lying in his bed. Our eyes met briefly but there was no sign of recognition in his dull face. Instead, he rolled away from me and asked:

"Where is your son?"

I crossed the room and knelt by his bed. I was afraid to touch him for fear of disturbing his wounds or tormenting his aching soul even more. He clutched his side as if his ribs hurt badly and I could see that his face was bruised and swollen.

"I am alone," I answered, swallowing back my tears. "Who did this to you?"

"Dich." (The enemy.) It was a peasant's standard answer.

I went to the kitchen and made some tea from a few dried leaves. It was as if my father knew he was dying and did not wish the house or its stores to survive him. If one must die alone, it should be in an empty place without wasting a thing.

When I returned, he was on his back. I held his poor, scabbed head and helped him drink some tea. I could see he was dehydrated, being unable to draw water from the well or get up to drink it even when neighbors brought some to the house.

"Where were you taken? What was the charge?" I asked.

"It doesn't matter." My father drank gratefully and lay back on the bed. "The Americans came to examine our family bunker. Because it was so big, they thought Viet Cong might be hiding inside and ordered me to go in first. When I came out and told them no one was there, they didn't believe me and threw in some grenades. One of them didn't go off right away and the two Americans who went in afterward were killed. They were just boys—" My father coughed up blood. "I don't blame them for being angry. That's what war is all about, isn't it? Bad luck. Bad karma."

"So they beat you up?"

"They pinned a paper on my back that said 'VC' and took me to Hoa Cam District for interrogation. I don't have to tell you what happened after that. I'm just lucky to be alive. . . . "

Because the Americans so dominated the area, I felt comparatively safe staying near my house and tending to my father. Unlike the Republicans, who **commandeered**[1] civilian houses for their quarters, the Americans kept their distance and so managed to avoid a lot of friction

---

[1] **commandeered**—seized for military use; confiscated.

with the peasants. I no longer tried to sell anything (the villagers still hated anyone who dealt with the invaders) and pretended I didn't speak English when their troops stopped me from time to time. Although people going to the toilet or gathering firewood were still shot occasionally by jumpy soldiers, things remained blessedly quiet. It had been months since a major Viet Cong attack and a new, if smaller, generation of children now played in Ky La's streets. More dangerous were the Koreans who now patrolled the American sector. Because a child from our village once walked into their camp and exploded a Viet Cong bomb wired to his body, the Koreans took terrible **retribution**[2] against the children themselves (whom they saw simply as little Viet Cong). After the incident, some Korean soldiers went to a school, snatched up some boys, threw them into a well, and tossed a grenade in afterward as an example to the others. To the villagers, these Koreans were like the Moroccans—tougher and meaner than the white soldiers they supported. Like the Japanese of World War II, they seemed to have no conscience and went about their duties as ruthless killing machines. No wonder they found my country a perfect place to ply their terrible trade.

I discovered that most of the kids I grew up with (those who had not been killed in the fighting) had married or moved away. Girls my age, if they had not yet married, were considered burdens on their family—old maids who consumed food without producing children. They also attracted the unsavory attention of soldiers, which always led to trouble. One reason so many of our young women wound up in the cities was because the shortage of available men made them liabilities to their families. At least a dutiful grown-up daughter could work as a housekeeper,

---

[2] **retribution**—something given in repayment, especially punishment.

nanny, hostess, or prostitute and send back money to the family who no longer wanted her. Many families, too, had been uprooted—like the refugees from Bai Gian or those who had been moved so that their houses could be bulldozed to provide a better fire zone for the Americans. For every soldier who went to battle, a hundred civilians moved ahead of him—to get out of the way; or behind him—following in his wake the way leaves are pulled along in a cyclone, hoping to live off his garbage, his money, and when all else failed, his mercy.

This is not to say that rubble and refugees were the only by-products of our war. Hundreds of thousands of tons of rice and countless motorbikes, luxury cars, TVs, stereos, refrigerators, air conditioners, and crates of cigarettes, liquor, and cosmetics were imported for the Vietnamese elite and the Americans who supported them. This created a new class of privileged people—wealthy young officers, officials, and war profiteers—who supplanted the elderly as objects of **veneration.**[3] Consequently, displaced farmers—old people, now, as well as young—became their servants, working as maids to the madams or bootblacks for fuzz-cheeked GIs. It was a common sight to see old people prostrate themselves before these young **demigods,**[4] crying *lay ong*—I beg you, sir!—where before such elderly people paid homage to no one but their ancestors. It was a world turned on its head.

Of those villagers who remained in Ky La, many were disfigured from the war, suffering amputated limbs, jagged scars, or the diseases that followed malnutrition or took over a body no longer inhabited by a happy human spirit.

---

[3] **veneration**—profound respect or reverence.

[4] **demigods**—people who are highly honored or revered.

Saddest of all these, perhaps, was Ong Xa Quang, a once-wealthy man who had been like a second father to me in the village. Quang was a handsome, good-natured man who sent two sons north in 1954. Of his two remaining sons, one was drafted by the Republican army and the other, much later, joined the Viet Cong. His two daughters married men who also went north, and so were left widows for at least the duration of the war. When I went to visit Quang I found his home and his life in ruins. He had lost both legs to an American mine, and every last son had been killed in battle. His wife now neglected him (she wasn't home when I called) because he was so much trouble to care for and he looked malnourished and on the verge of starvation. Still, he counted himself lucky. Fate had spared his life while it took the lives of so many others around him. All his suffering was part of his life's education—but for what purpose, he admitted he was still not wise enough to know. Nonetheless, Quang said I should remember everything he told me, and to forget none of the details of the tragedies I myself had seen and was yet to see. I gave him a daughter's tearful hug and left, knowing I would probably never see him alive again.

I walked to the hill behind my house where my father had taken me when I was a little girl—the hill where he told me about my destiny and duty as a Phung Thi woman. I surveyed the broken dikes and battered crops and empty animal pens of my once flourishing village. I saw the ghosts of my friends and relatives going about their work and a generation of children who would never be born playing in the muddy fields and dusty streets. I wondered about the martyrs and heroes of our ancient legends—shouldn't they be here to throw back the invaders and punish the Vietnamese on both sides who were making our country not just a graveyard, but a sewer of corruption and prison of fear? Could a god who made such saints as well as ordinary people truly be a god if he couldn't feel our suffering with us? For that matter, what use was god at all when people, not deities, seemed to cause our problems on earth?

I shut my eyes and called on my spirit sense to answer but I heard no reply. It was as if life's cycle was no longer birth, growth, and death but only endless dying brought about by endless war. I realized that I, along with so many of my countrymen, had been born into war and that my soul knew nothing else. I tried to imagine people somewhere who knew only peace— what a paradise! How many souls in that world were blessed with the simple privilege of saying good-bye to their loved ones before they died? And how many of those loved ones died with the smile of a life well lived on their lips—knowing that their existence added up to something more than a number in a "body count" or another human brick on a towering wall of corpses? Perhaps such a place was America, although American wives and mothers, too, were losing husbands and sons every day in the evil **vortex**[5] between heaven and hell that my country had become.

I sat on the hill for a very long time, like a vessel waiting to be filled up with rain—soft wisdom from heaven—but the sun simply drifted lower in the west and the insects buzzed and the tin roofs of the American camp shimmered in the heat and my village and the war sat heavily—unmoved and unmovable like an oppressive gravestone—on my land and in my heart. I got up and dusted off my pants. It was time to feed my father.

Back home, I told him about my visit to "our hilltop." I said I now regretted fleeing Ky La. Perhaps it would have been better to stay and fight—to fight the Americans with the Viet Cong or the Viet Cong with the Republicans or to fight both together by myself and with anyone else who would join me.

---

[5] **vortex**—whirlpool.

My father stopped eating and looked at me intently. "Bay Ly, you were born to be a wife and mother, not a killer. That is your duty. For as long as you live, you must remember what I say. You and me—we weren't born to make enemies. Don't make vengeance your god, because such gods are satisfied only by human sacrifice."

"But there has been so much suffering—so much destruction!" I replied, again on the verge of tears, "Shouldn't someone be punished?"

"Are you so smart that you truly know who's to blame? If you ask the Viet Cong, they'll blame the Americans. If you ask the Americans, they'll blame the North. If you ask the North, they'll blame the South. If you ask the South, they'll blame the Viet Cong. If you ask the monks, they'll blame the Catholics, or tell you our ancestors did something terrible and so brought this endless suffering on our heads. So tell me, who would you punish? The common soldier on both sides who's only doing his duty? Would you ask the French or Americans to repay our Vietnamese debt?"

"But generals and politicians give orders—orders to kill and destroy. And our own people cheat each other as if there's nothing to it. I know—I've seen it! And nobody has the right to destroy Mother Earth!"

"Well then, Bay Ly, go out and do the same, eh? Kill the killers and cheat the cheaters. That will certainly stop the war, won't it? Perhaps that's been our problem all along—not enough profiteers and soldiers!"

Despite my father's reasoning, my anger and confusion were so full-up that they burst forth, not with new arguments, but tears. He took me in his arms. "Shhh— listen, little peach blossom, when you see all those young Americans out there being killed and wounded in our war—in a war that fate or luck or god has commanded us to wage for our redemption and education—you must thank them, at least in your heart, for helping to put us back on our life's course. Don't wonder about right and wrong. Those are weapons as deadly as bombs and bullets. Right is the goodness you carry in your heart—love for your ancestors and your baby and your family and for everything that lives. Wrong is anything that comes between you and that love. Go back to your little son. Raise him the best way you can. That is the battle you were born to fight. That is the victory you must win."

QUESTIONS TO CONSIDER

1. Why is Le Ly so frightened by the loss of her village's temples, pagodas, and shrines?

2. Why was Le Ly's father beaten?

3. Le Ly calls Vietnam an evil place "between heaven and hell." What does she mean?

4. According to her father, Le Ly must concentrate on only one battle. What is it?

War from the Air

Bombs Away A U.S. Air Force F-100 drops bombs on the Mekong Delta in 1965.

▲

Over the Jungle An A-1 Skyraider bombs the jungles of South Vietnam.

Explosion A phosphorous bomb explodes in a village near Ca Mau.

▲

Bombing Hanoi Smoke rises from a rail yard in Hanoi, which was hit by U.S. fighter bombers.

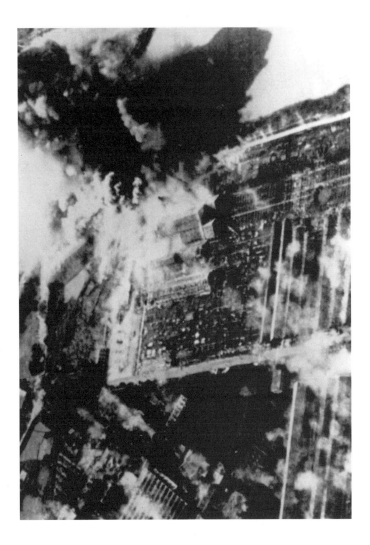

▲
Bombing Hanoi II U.S. bombs hitting a bridge near Hanoi in 1967.

Bombing a Village An A-1 Skyraider bombs a village in the Mekong Delta.

Dissent at Home

Part four

Resisting the Draft

In the spring of 1965 when Lyndon Johnson began escalating the war, the antiwar movement in the United States also began to take shape. At first it was mainly small demonstrations against the decision to bomb North Vietnam. In the summer of 1965, a new form of protest arose: the burning of draft cards. This was an act of public defiance that generally led to immediate imprisonment. Since 1948, every eighteen-year-old man had to register for the draft. When soldiers were needed, some of the registered men were called up for military service. The burning of a draft card was a criminal act, but also a potent form of protest. On October 16, 1967, the Resistance, an organization opposed to the war, began a national campaign of refusal to respond to the draft. The "Declaration of Conscience" is a pledge by students not to serve if drafted, and "We Refuse" is a statement put out by the Resistance group during its anti-draft campaign.

Declaration of Conscience Against the War in Vietnam

We the undersigned, are young Americans of draft age. We understand our obligations to defend our country and to serve in the armed forces but we object to being asked to support the war in South Vietnam.

Believing the United States' participation in the war is for the suppression of the Vietnamese struggle for national independence, we see no justification for our involvement. We agree with Senator Wayne Morse, who said on the floor of the Senate on March 4, 1964, regarding South Vietnam, that "We should never have gone in. We should never have stayed in. We should get out."

Believing that we should not be asked to fight against the people of Vietnam, we herewith state our refusal to do so.

We Refuse

The Resistance is a group of men who are bound together by one single and clear commitment: on October 16 we will hand in our draft cards and refuse any further cooperation with the Selective Service System. By doing so we will actively challenge the government's right to draft American men for its criminal war against the people of Vietnam. We of the Resistance feel that we can no longer passively acquiesce to the Selective Service System by accepting its deferments. The American military system depends upon students, those opposed to war, and those with anti-Vietnam war politics wrangling for the respective deferments. Those opposed to the war are dealt with quietly, individually and on the government's terms. If they do not get the deferments, they must individually find some extra-legal alternative. A popular last resort is Canada, and those who go to Canada must be politically silent in order to stay there. Legal draft alternatives are kept within reach of elite groups— good students, those who are able to express objection to all war on religious grounds, and those with the money to hire good lawyers. For the majority of American guys the only alternatives are jail or the army. While those who are most opposed to the war have been silenced, the system that provides the personnel for war crimes continues to function smoothly.

Many who wish to avoid the draft will, of course, choose to accept deferments; many, however, wish to do more than avoid the draft. Resistance means that if the government is to continue its crimes against humanity, it must first deal with our opposition. We do not seek jail, but we do this because as individuals we know of no justifiable alternative and we believe that in time many other American men will also choose to resist the crimes done in their names.

QUESTIONS TO CONSIDER

1. What is the Resistance?

2. Why do the men of the Resistance refuse to be drafted?

3. Do you agree or disagree with these men's decision to resist the draft? Explain.

Two Poems

In 1965, a twelve-year-old girl named Barbara Beidler, from Florida, sent a poem about the Vietnam War to Venture *magazine. The poem "Afterthoughts on a Napalm-Drop on Jungle Villages near Haiphong" was a potent and obvious protest against the war and the damage done to civilian Vietnamese. Napalm is a highly flammable, jelly-like substance used in* **incendiary**[1] *bombs; dropped on the ground it burns out enemy positions or villages. Beidler's poem caused a national scandal. The Vietnamese poet Huy Can wrote "Truth Blazes Even in Little Children's Hearts" in response to Beidler's poem.*

---

[1] **incendiary**—causing or capable of causing fire.

Afterthoughts on a Napalm-Drop on Jungle Villages near Haiphong

BY BARBARA BEIDLER

All was still.
The sun rose through silver pine boughs,
Over sleeping green-straw huts,
Over cool rice ponds,
Through the emerald jungles.
Into the sky.

The men rose and went out to the fields and ponds.
The women set pots on the fire, boiling rice and jungle
    berries, and some with baskets went for fish.
The children played in the streams and danced
    through the weeds.

Then there was the flash—silver and gold
Silver and gold,
Silver birds flying,
Golden water raining.
The rice ponds blazed with the new water.
The jungles burst into gold and sent up little birds of
    fire.
Little animals with fur of flame.

Then the children flamed.
Running—their clothes flying like fiery kites.
Screaming—their screams dying as their faces **seared**.[2]
The women's baskets burned on their heads.
The men's blazed on the rice waters.

---

[2] **seared**—charred, scorched, or burned.

Then the rains came.
A rag, fire black, fluttered.
A curl of smoke rose from a lone rice stem.
The forest lay singed, seared.
A hut crumbled.

And all was still.
　　　　Listen, Americans,
　　　　Listen, clear and long.
　　　　The children are screaming
　　　　In the jungles of Haiphong.

Truth Blazes Even in Little Children's Hearts

BY HUY CAN

Little Barbara
Separated from us by the ocean
And by the color of your skin
You have heard and understood.

You have heard the screams
Of the children near Haiphong
Whose clothing turns to flame
From American napalm.

You are twelve years old
And your heart speaks
For the conscience of mankind
Tormented by each rain of bombs.

America, America!
Don't you hear the screams
Of those thousands of children

Consumed by the golden fire?
Golden fire of napalm
Golden fire of dollars
Which eats the flesh
Like a cancer.

A filthy cancer
Devouring the bones
The blood and the soul
Of the United States.

America, don't you feel
The fire burning your flesh
And your conscience
Killed by your bombs?

Little Barbara,
The fire of your poem
Scorches the demons
And drives them wild.

They would ban poetry
But how can they ban
The truth that blazes
Even in little children's hearts!

QUESTIONS TO CONSIDER

1. What clues can you find that "Afterthoughts on a Napalm-Drop" is a poem of protest?

2. What did Huy Can want Americans to do about the war?

3. Reread stanza six of "Truth Blazes." How is the Vietnam War like "a filthy cancer"?

The Whole World Was Watching

BY LANCE MORROW

In March 1968, Lyndon Johnson, tired by the war and by the protests in the U.S., announced that he would not run again for president. The campaign for the Democratic party nomination over the summer was a fierce one between traditional Democrats and the young radicals. This conflict finally spilled over at the Democratic Convention in Chicago. Here, peaceful protests were turned into violent melees by riot police. With the cameras rolling, the police beat the protesters and shocked the whole nation. The following account of the riots was written in 1996 by Lance Morrow when the Democrats returned again to Chicago for their convention.

Outside the Hilton, at the corner of Michigan Avenue and Balbo Drive, I stood talking to Winston Spencer Churchill. Churchill was kicking around the world as a correspondent. I noticed he liked to watch the reaction when he stuck out his hand and said, "Hullo, I'm Winston Churchill." For he resembled his grandfather's pictures taken when that young Winston

covered the Boer War at the turn of the century—
boyish and freckled, greedy for trouble. Now, behind
the police lines, Churchill and I chatted with a guilty,
voyeur's[1] air, as if awaiting some illegal sporting event—
a cockfight or a sloppily organized human sacrifice.

It was early evening on Wednesday, just after 7.
Even on the lakefront, the air stank. The tear gas dispensed by one side and the stink bombs set off by
the other lingered in mouth and throat. Across the
scene (**phalanxes**[2] of blue-helmeted cops, battle jeeps
with barbed wire like mustaches across their grilles, the
guerrilla-idealist young in tantrum, their faces contorted
with rage) there swept not only rhythmic waves of
sound ("Hey, Hey, L.B.J., how many kids did you kill
today?") but an amazing Satanic smell, a Yippie genius'
brew that simulated vomit, decomposing flesh, death,
cloaca[3] and kindred flavors. It was what evil would
smell like if it were available in an aerosol can—bad
enough to make the South Side stockyards, next door to
the convention, smell almost wholesome. This exotic
moral stink had drifted halfway around the world, after
all, from Vietnam.

In front of the Hilton, on Michigan Avenue, two
sides of America ground against each other like tectonic
plates.[4] Each side cartooned and ridiculed the other so
brutally that by now the two seemed to belong almost
to different species. The '60s had a genius for excess
and caricature. On one side, the love-it-or-leave-it, proud,
Middle American, Okie-from-Muskogee, traditionalist
nation of squares who supported the cold war assump-
tions that took Lyndon Johnson ever deeper into
Vietnam. On the other side, the "countercultural" young,

---

[1] **voyeur's**—like that of an obsessive observer of sordid or sensational subjects.

[2] **phalanxes**—compact or close-knit groups of people.

[3] cloaca—a sewer or latrine.

[4] tectonic plates—the drifting, continent-sized segments that make up the earth's crust.

either flower children or revolutionaries, and their fellow-traveling adult allies in the antiwar movement, the Eugene McCarthy uprising against L.B.J., people whose hatred of the war in Vietnam led them into ever greater alienation from American society and its figures of authority.

Mayor Richard Daley's front-line forces in Chicago must have been chosen for immovable heft, men built like trucks. Now they silently palm-smacked their clubs, their eyes as narrow as the slits in an armored car. Most of the convention delegates and dignitaries quartered in the fortress Hilton were at the moment three miles away at the convention hall, preparing to bestow upon poor Hubert Humphrey the nomination he thought would redeem the years of humiliation and corrupting self-abasement he had endured as Johnson's Vice President.

The police needed to protect the Hilton nonetheless. It housed not only delegates and candidates but also the country's **besieged**[5] political process, its apparently crumbling legitimacy. Recollect the famous sequence at the front end of 1968, that bizarre and violent year:

> 1) The war that America was fighting for inaccessible reasons in an obscure little Southeast Asian country seemed to blow up in America's face with the communists' Tet offensive in late January.

> 2) Minnesota's Democratic Senator, Eugene McCarthy, challenged his President, Lyndon Johnson, in the New Hampshire primary and won 42.4% of the Democratic vote. Seeing that, Robert Kennedy hurried into the race.

---

[5] **besieged**—overwhelmed.

3) L.B.J. withdrew as a candidate for re-election.

4) Martin Luther King Jr. was assassinated, a murder that precipitated days of riots in cities across the country.

5) Robert Kennedy was killed in Los Angeles in early June. And so on. It is a part of the folklore, each act more amazing than the one before, a dark jack-in-the-box of history. On Tuesday night of the Democratic Convention week, the Soviets invaded Czechoslovakia and eradicated the "Prague spring."

Now there was silence on the cops' side of the barricades—an ominous, hurricane stillness. On the other side: the dirty, skinny, red-eyed, hyper, unslept, screaming, antiwar young, their youthful energy converted to electrical fury. Rage shot out of them like sparks, like flaming snakes. No flowers in their hair now. The foresighted wore football helmets.

Then the cops charged. They moved with surprising speed and a nimble fury like that of a rhinoceros attacking. A flying wedge of blue drove down Balbo into the noisy, ragged flesh on Michigan. The cops bent to their work, avengers at harvest time, chop-swinging clubs with methodical ferocity, a burst-boil rage. And in the midst of it, I began to detect a certain professional satisfaction of the kind a hitter feels sometimes. The cops had found a ghastly sweet spot. The sound that a club makes when it strikes a human skull—in earnest—awakens in the hearer a sickened, fearful amazement. No kidding now: a thunk! **resonant**[6] through the skull and its wet package of thought and immortal soul.

---

[6] **resonant**—strong and deep in tone; resounding.

It dawned on me that I was now an animal as much in season as the protesters, for the blue rhino was wheeling back, flailing through the bloodied crowd. I skittered into the Hilton lobby. A cop lumbered after me with club upraised and aimed at my skull just above the left ear. I held up my press credentials like a ridiculous little magic shield, like a clove of garlic or the sign of the cross, and the cop went into freeze-frame and thought about the matter long and hard before at last he lowered his club, a flicker of disappointment in his eye, and moved on to hunt for other game deeper in the lobby.

The cops outside went on banging heads almost indiscriminately. Middle-aged bystanders were as likely to be bloodied as young radicals. People were dragged feetfirst, heads bouncing on pavement, to paddy wagons and hurled in.

The demonstrators knew their McLuhan[7] and chanted, "The whole world is watching." After a delay caused by strikes that prevented live transmission, the television networks finally broadcast the footage of what a national commission would later call a "police riot." Uncle Walter Cronkite was visibly furious. Tom Wicker would write in the *New York Times*, "Those were our children in the streets, and the Chicago police beat them up."

The bashing on Michigan Avenue was only one of a series that week. In the last, just before dawn on Friday after the convention adjourned, the police permitted themselves to go berserk in the halls of the Hilton, rousting sleeping McCarthy workers from their rooms and beating on their skulls. Police claimed

---

[7] McLuhan—a reference to Marshall McLuhan (1911–1980), the Canadian writer and teacher who generated widespread controversy during the 1960s with his theories of the effects of the media on society.

the workers had been throwing things (beer cans, ashtrays, bags of excrement) down on cops from the windows above.

The 1968 Democratic Convention was part of the Ur-mess[8] of the '60s and in a sense the Big Bang of the American culture wars. And here we are in 1996: more or less the same two tectonic plates are still grinding against each other in America. Their surfaces may be a little smoother now.

Before Johnson fell for the tar baby of Vietnam, Americans believed their Presidents almost always told them the truth. The level of trust and therefore respect for authority was probably foolishly high. All of that changed in the fatal asininity of Vietnam. The baby boomers' rites of passage turned into a huge Oedipal[9] overtoppling of authority, an assault on Dad that was disorientingly successful.

It takes years for all the myth and trauma to work through the system. Maybe they have done so only this summer, after 28 years have passed and the Democrats feel free, as adults now, leaders of the party, to return to the old slaughterhouse. This year the Democrats have conducted a lottery for groups that want to hold protests at their convention.

After the police charged on Michigan Avenue, I lost track of Churchill and did not see him again at the convention. Chicago that week was crawling with famous names, including an unusual number of literary celebrities, all bent on getting high on a snort of anti-Establishment danger and writing about it— Norman Mailer, Jean Genet, William Burroughs, Allen

---

[8] Ur-mess—the biggest or one of the first big messes.

[9] Oedipal—having to do with the Oedipus complex, a strong childhood attachment to the parent of the opposite sex, often accompanied by a feeling of rivalry, hostility, or fear toward the other parent.

Ginsburg, who went about dispensing his Buddhist "oms" through the tear gas. Next week the Chicago convention may run more to Hollywood celebrities. None will be teargassed.

QUESTIONS TO CONSIDER

1. Why do the police begin beating the protesters?

2. Why do the protesters chant "The whole world is watching"?

3. What about his story seems to anger Lance Morrow the most?

from

Born on the Fourth of July

BY RON KOVIC

*Ron Kovic volunteered for the Marines to go and fight in Vietnam.
He assumed that he was going off to fight for American values
as his father had done in World War II. Kovic, however, saw a war
of a very different kind in Vietnam before being wounded and
paralyzed. His experiences turned him against the war. From his
wheelchair, Kovic raised his voice in protest against the war, trying
to save other idealistic young men from his fate. In 1972, Kovic
attended the Republican National Convention in Miami Beach to
protest President Nixon's policies in Vietnam. Kovic published a
memoir,* Born on the Fourth of July, *in 1976; it was made into a
film in 1989. The following is Kovic's account of the 1972 protest
against Nixon.*

It was the night of Nixon's acceptance speech and
now I was on my own deep in his territory, all alone in
my wheelchair in a sweat-soaked marine utility jacket
covered with medals from the war. A TV producer I

knew from the Coast had gotten me past the guards at the entrance with his press pass. My eyes were still smarting from teargas. Outside the chain metal fence around the Convention Center my friends were being clubbed and arrested, herded into wagons. The crowds were thick all around me, people dressed as if they were going to a banquet, men in expensive summer suits and women in light elegant dresses. Every once in a while someone would look at me as if I didn't belong there. But I had come almost three thousand miles for this meeting with the president and nothing was going to prevent it from taking place.

I worked my way slowly and carefully into the huge hall, moving down one of the side aisles. "Excuse me, excuse me," I said to delegates as I pushed past them farther and farther to the front of the hall toward the speakers' podium.

I had gotten only halfway toward where I wanted to be when I was stopped by one of the convention security marshals. "Where are you going?" he said. He grabbed hold of the back of my chair, I made believe I hadn't heard him and kept turning my wheels, but his grip on the chair was too tight and now two other security men had joined him.

"What's the matter?" I said. "Can't a disabled veteran who fought for his country sit up front?"

The three men looked at each other for a moment and one of them said, "I'm afraid not. You're not allowed up front with the delegates." I had gotten as far as I had on sheer bluff alone and now they were telling me I could go no farther. "You'll have to go to the back of the convention hall, son. Let's go," said the guard who was holding my chair.

In a move of desperation I swung around facing all three of them, shouting as loud as I could so Walter Cronkite and the CBS camera crew that was just above me could hear me and maybe even focus their cameras in for the six o'clock news. "I'm a Vietnam veteran and I fought in the war! Did you fight in the war?"

One of the guards looked away.

"Yeah, that's what I thought," I said. "I bet none of you fought in the war and you guys are trying to throw me out of the convention. I've got just as much right to be up front here as any of these delegates. I fought for that right and I was born on the Fourth of July."

I was really shouting now and another officer came over. I think he might have been in charge of the hall. He told me I could stay where I was if I was quiet and didn't move up any farther. I agreed with the compromise. I locked my brakes and looked for other veterans in the tremendous crowd. As far as I could tell, I was the only one who had made it in.

People had begun to sit down all around me. They all had Four More Years buttons and I was surprised to see how many of them were young. I began speaking to them, telling them about the Last Patrol and why veterans from all over the United States had taken the time and effort to travel thousands of miles to the Republican National Convention. "I'm a disabled veteran!" I shouted. "I served two tours of duty in Vietnam and while on my second tour of duty up in the DMZ I was wounded and paralyzed from the chest down." I told them I would be that way for the rest of my life. Then I began to talk about the hospitals and how they treated the returning veterans like animals, how I, many nights in the Bronx, had lain in my own shit for hours waiting for an aide. "And they never come," I said. "They never come because that man that's going to accept the nomination tonight has been lying to all of us and spending the money on war that should be spent on healing and helping the wounded. That's the biggest lie and hypocrisy of all—

that we had to go over there and fight and get crippled and come home to a government and leaders who could care less about the same boys they sent over."

I kept shouting and speaking, looking for some kind of reaction from the crowd. No one seemed to want to even look at me.

"Is it too real for you to look at? Is this wheelchair too much for you to take? The man who will accept the nomination tonight is a liar!" I shouted again and again, until finally one of the security men came back and told me to be quiet or they would have to take me to the back of the hall.

I told him that if they tried to move me or touch my chair there would be a fight and hell to pay right there in front of Walter Cronkite and the national television networks. I told him if he wanted to wrestle me and beat me to the floor of the convention hall in front of all those cameras he could.

By then a couple of newsmen, including Roger Mudd from CBS, had worked their way through the security barricades and begun to ask me questions.

"Why are you here tonight?" Roger Mudd asked me. "But don't start talking until I get the camera here," he shouted.

It was too good to be true. In a few seconds Roger Mudd and I would be going on live all over the country. I would be doing what I had come here for, showing the whole nation what the war was all about. The camera began to roll, and I began to explain why I and the others had come, that the war was wrong and it had to stop immediately. "I'm a Vietnam veteran," I said. "I gave America my all and the leaders of this government threw me and the others away to rot in their V.A. hospitals. What's happening in Vietnam is a crime against humanity, and I just want the American people to know that we have come all the way across this country, sleeping on the ground and in the rain, to let the American people see for themselves the men who fought their war and have come to oppose it. If you can't believe the veteran who fought the war and was wounded in the war, who can you believe?"

"Thank you," said Roger Mudd, visibly moved by what I had said. "This is Roger Mudd," he said, "down on the convention floor with Ron Kovic, a disabled veteran protesting President Nixon's policy in Vietnam.". . .

Suddenly a roar went up in the convention hall, louder than anything I had ever heard in my life. It started off as a rumble, then gained in intensity until it sounded like a tremendous thunderbolt. "Four more years, four more years," the crowd roared over and over again. The fat woman next to me was jumping up and down and dancing in the aisle. It was the greatest ovation the president of the United States had ever received and he loved it. I held the sides of my wheelchair to keep my hands from shaking. After what seemed forever, the roar finally began to die down.

This was the moment I had come three thousand miles for, this was it, all the pain and the rage, all the trials and the death of the war and what had been done to me and a generation of Americans by all the men who had lied to us and tricked us, by the man who stood before us in the convention hall that night, while men who had fought for their country were being gassed and beaten in the street outside the hall. I thought of Bobby who sat next to me and the months we had spent in the hospital in the Bronx. It was all hitting me at once, all those years, all that destruction, all that sorrow.

President Nixon began to speak and all three of us took a deep breath and shouted at the top of our lungs, "Stop the bombing, stop the war, stop the bombing, stop the war," as loud and as hard as we could, looking directly at Nixon. The security agents immediately threw up their arms, trying to hide us from the cameras and the president. "Stop the bombing, stop the bombing," I screamed. For an instant Cronkite looked down, then turned his head away. They're not going to show it, I thought. They're going to try and hide us like they did in the hospitals. Hundreds of people around us began to clap and shout "Four more years," trying to drown out our protest. They all seemed very angry and shouted at us to stop. We continued shouting, interrupting Nixon again and again until Secret Service agents grabbed our chairs from behind and began pulling us backward as fast as they could out of the convention hall. "Take it easy," Bobby said to me. "Don't fight back."

I wanted to take a swing and fight right there in the middle of the convention hall in front of the president and the whole country. "So this is how they treat their wounded veterans!" I screamed.

A short guy with a big Four More Years button ran up to me and spat in my face. "Traitor!" he screamed, as he was yanked back by police. **Pandemonium**[1] was breaking out all around us and the Secret Service men kept pulling us out backward.

"I served two tours of duty in Vietnam!" I screamed to one newsman. "I gave three-quarters of my body for America. And what do I get? Spit in the face!" I kept screaming until we hit the side entrance where the agents pushed us outside and shut the doors, locking them with chains and padlocks so reporters wouldn't be able to follow us out for interviews.

---

[1] **pandemonium**—wild uproar or noise.

All three of us sat holding on to each other shaking. We had done it. It had been the biggest moment of our lives, we had shouted down the president of the United States and disrupted his acceptance speech. What more was there left to do but go home?

I sat in my chair still shaking and began to cry.

QUESTIONS TO CONSIDER

1. Why does Kovic believe that the government doesn't care about the boys sent to fight in Vietnam?

2. Why does Kovic cry after he has been thrown out of the convention hall?

3. If you had been at the convention, would you have wanted to listen to Kovic? Why or why not?

Songs of the War

The divided American opinion of the war in Vietnam is very well depicted in the popular music of the time. Rock and folk music were important vehicles of the protest movement, but popular music did also support the soldiers in Vietnam. "The Ballad of the Green Berets" was written by a Special Forces officer and was the most popular song in America in 1966. It expresses a heroic view of the war. Country Joe McDonald's "I-Feel-Like-I'm-Fixin'-to-Die Rag" is a protest song that became an anthem of the antiwar movement at Woodstock in 1969. It attacks the government for failing to justify sending young men to die. "Fortunate Son" by Creedence Clearwater Revival is another protest against the draft, particularly the exemptions that allowed college students to defer their call-up. These deferments led to the sense that the sons of well-to-do Americans were able to escape service and only the poor had to fight.

The Ballad of the Green Berets

BY BARRY SADLER AND ROBIN MOORE

Fighting soldiers from the sky,
Fearless men who jump and die.
Men who mean just what they say,
The brave men of The Green Beret.

Silver wings upon their chests,
These are men, America's best.
One hundred men we'll test today,
But only three win The Green Beret.

Trained to live off nature's land,
Trained to combat, hand to hand.
Men who fight by night and day,
Courage take from The Green Beret.

Silver wings upon their chests,
These are men, America's best.
One hundred men we'll test today,
But only three win The Green Beret.

Back at home a young wife waits
Her Green Beret has met his fate.
He has died for those oppressed,
Leaving her his last request.

Put silver wings on my son's chest,
Make him one of America's best.
He'll be a man they'll test one day.
Have him win The Green Beret.

I-Feel-Like-I'm-Fixin'-to-Die Rag

BY COUNTRY JOE MCDONALD

Come on all of you big strong men,
Uncle Sam needs your help again;
He's got himself in a terrible jam
Way down yonder in Viet Nam;
So put down your books and pick up a gun,
We're gonna have a whole lot of fun!

Chorus:
And it's one two three,
What are we fighting for?
Don't ask me, I don't give·a damn,
Next stop is Vietnam.
And it's five six seven,
Open up the Pearly Gates;
There ain't no time to wonder why,
Whoopie—we're all gonna die!

Come on, generals, let's move fast,
Your big chance has come at last;
Now you can go out and get those Reds,
The only good Commie is one that's dead;
You know that peace can only be won,
When we've blown 'em all to kingdom come!

(Chorus)

Come on, Wall Street, don't be slow,
Why, man, this is war Au-go-go;
There's plenty good money to be made,
Supplying the army with tools of the trade;
Just hope and pray if they drop the Bomb,
They drop it on the Viet Cong!

(Chorus)

Come on, mothers, throughout the land,
Pack your boys off to Vietnam;
Come on, fathers, don't hesitate,
Send your sons off before it's too late;
You can be the first one on your block
To have your boy come home in a box.

(Chorus)

Fortunate Son

**BY CREEDENCE CLEARWATER REVIVAL/
JOHN FOGERTY**

Some folks are born made to wave the flag;
ooh, they're red, white and blue.

And when the band plays "Hail to the chief,"
they point the cannon right at you.

It ain't me, it ain't me—I ain't no senator's son.
It ain't me, it ain't me;—I ain't no fortunate one. one. one.

Some folks are born, silver spoon in hand;
Lord, don't they help themselves.

But when the tax man comes to the door,
Lord, the house looks like a rummage sale.

It ain't me, it ain't me—I ain't no millionaire's son.
It ain't me, it ain't me;—I ain't no fortunate one. one. one.

Some folks inherit star spangled eyes;
ooh, they send you down to war.

And when you ask them, "How much should we give?"
they only answer More! more! more!

It ain't me, it ain't me—I ain't no military son.
It ain't me, it ain't me;—I ain't no fortunate one. one. one.

QUESTIONS TO CONSIDER

1. What is the dying soldier's last request in "The Ballad of the Green Berets"?

2. Why is the speaker of "I-Feel-Like-I'm-Fixin'-to-Die" bitter?

3. What does the line "I ain't no fortunate one" mean?

The Antiwar
Movement

Protesting at the Pentagon In October 1967, there was a huge antiwar demonstration at the Pentagon outside Washington, D.C.

▲

The 1968 Democratic Convention Delegates raising placards to show their support for candidate Eugene McCarthy and his promise to end the war in Vietnam.

Stop the War An antiwar demonstration held outside the 1968 Democratic Convention in Chicago.

▼

▲
Burning Draft Cards At an antiwar demonstration, eligible young men
burn their draft cards.

◀ **At the Capitol** Protestors gather at the Capitol in Washington, D.C.

Living Room War Americans watched much of the Vietnam War unfold on television.
▼

Kent State A headline from *The Washington Post*
describes the killing of four student protestors
at Kent State University by National Guardsmen in
1970. Below students stage an antiwar demonstration, carrying wooden boxes to symbolize all of
those who have died.
▼

Chapter 44

The Tet Offensive
and the American
Withdrawal

Not a Dove, But No Longer a Hawk

BY NEIL SHEEHAN

As U.S. military escalation failed to bring the promised results, or even move the U.S. closer to victory, many people began to re-evaluate the war and why they were there. Neil Sheehan had arrived in Vietnam in 1962 to cover the war, fully certain of the need for U.S. intervention in Vietnam. Four years later, Sheehan was reconsidering this certainty. Corruption, military incompetence, and the lack of any real attempt to combat the appeal of the Viet Cong were forcing people like Sheehan to see America's role in Vietnam as at best misguided, and at worst colonial, like the French before them.

Americans, because they are Americans, arrive in Vietnam full of enthusiasm and with the best of intentions. After a prolonged period of residence, they leave with their enthusiasm a victim of the cynicism that pervades Vietnamese life and with their good intentions lost somewhere in a paddy field. I am no exception.

When I first walked across the tarmac of Saigon's Tansonnhut Airport on a warm evening in April, 1962, nervous that the customs officers might not accept the journalist's visa I had hurriedly obtained from the South Vietnamese consulate in Hong Kong, I believed in what my country was doing in Vietnam. With military and economic aid and a few thousand pilots and Army advisers, the United States was attempting to help the non-Communist Vietnamese build a **viable**[1] and independent nation-state and defeat a Communist guerrilla insurgency that would subject them to a **dour**[2] tyranny. This seemed to me a worthy cause and something that needed to be done if other Southeast Asian peoples were to be allowed some freedom of choice in determining their course in history. Although I often disagreed with the implementation of American policy during my first two years in Vietnam, I was in accord with its basic aims.

I remember distinctly the thrill of climbing aboard a U.S. Army helicopter in the cool of the morning and taking off across the rice fields with a South Vietnamese battalion for a day's jousting with the Vietcong guerrillas. There was hope then that the non-Communist Vietnamese might win their war. I was proud of the young American pilots sitting at the controls in the cockpit and I was grateful for the opportunity to witness this adventure and to report it. We are fighting now, I used to think, and some day we will triumph and this will be a better country.

There were many disappointments those first two years, but when I left Vietnam in 1964, I was still, to use the current **parlance**,[3] a hawk. I returned to Saigon in 1965 for another year. Now I have left again, and much

---

[1] **viable**—capable of living, developing, or germinating under favorable conditions.

[2] **dour**—stern or forbidding.

[3] **parlance**—manner of speaking; idiom.

has changed. There were 17,000 American servicemen in Vietnam at the time of my first departure and there are now 317,000 and I, while not a dove, am no longer a hawk.

If I had been wiser and could have foreseen the present consequences of that earlier and relatively small-scale American intervention in the affairs of this country, I doubt that I would have been enthusiastic during those first two years. I realize now, perhaps because this past year has impressed upon me more forcefully the realities of the war and of Vietnamese society, that I was naive in believing the non-Communist Vietnamese could defeat the Communist insurgency and build a decent and progressive social structure. . . .

The flow of refugees from the countryside is the most eloquent evidence available of the gradual destruction of rural society under the impact of the war. The number of refugees has now passed the million mark. It takes a great deal to make a Vietnamese peasant forsake his land and the graves of his ancestors.

Most refugees I have questioned told me that the Vietcong taxed them and made them work harder than usual, but that they could live with the Communists. They left their homes, they said, because they could no longer bear American and South Vietnamese bombs and shells.

If resettled properly, the refugees could conceivably develop into an asset for the Saigon Government. Yet, true to its usual behavior, the regime neglects them and the majority are left to shift for themselves. Refugee slums have risen in the cities almost as fast as G.I. bars.

Deserted hamlets and barren rice fields, now a common sight, are other evidence of what the war is doing to rural South Vietnam. In several provinces on the northern central coast as much as one-third of the rice land has been forsaken. The American policy of killing crops in Communist-held areas by spraying them with chemical **defoliants**[4] from aircraft is hastening this process. During the first six months of this year 59,000 acres were destroyed.

The corrosive effect on the country of the American presence is not confined to military operations. Economically and culturally, the advent of the Americans has introduced **maladies**[5] only time can cure. One is inflation. The primitive economy, already seriously disrupted by the war, has now been swamped by the purchasing power of tens of millions of dollars being dispensed for the construction of bases, airfields and port facilities and by the free spending of the individual American soldier.

This year the United States will pump a minimum of $140-million into the Vietnamese economy to cover the locally generated costs of the construction of new bases and the maintenance of existing ones. This sum constitutes about one-seventh of the country's entire money supply. American troops are themselves currently spending another $7-million a month.

The moral degeneration caused by the G.I. culture that has mushroomed in the cities and towns is another malady. Bars and bordellos, thousands of young Vietnamese women degrading themselves as bar girls and prostitutes, gangs of hoodlums and beggars and children selling their older sisters and picking pockets have become **ubiquitous**[6] features of urban life. I have sometimes thought, when a street urchin with sores covering his legs, stopped me and begged for a few cents' worth of Vietnamese piastres, that he might be better off growing up as a political commissar. He would then, at least, have some self-respect.

---

[4] **defoliants**—chemicals sprayed or dusted on plants to cause the leaves to fall off.

[5] **maladies**—diseases, disorders, ailments.

[6] **ubiquitous**—being or seeming to be everywhere at the same time; omnipresent.

Rarely in any war has the name of the people been evoked more by both sides than in the Vietnam conflict. Yet the Vietnamese peasantry, who serve as cannon fodder[7] for Communists and non-Communists, remain curiously mute—a hushed Greek chorus to their own tragedy.

The conditions of life in Vietnam will probably always make an accurate assessment of the peasants' attitudes toward the war impossible to obtain. I have received the impression, however, on visits to accessible hamlets, that many of the peasants are so weary of the fighting they would accept any settlement that brought them peace.

Last March, I spent two days in one hamlet south of the port of Danang on the central coast. A company of U.S. Marines had seized the hamlet from the Vietcong six months previously, and a Government pacification team, protected by the Marines, was working there. In three years, the hamlet had changed hands three times. There were almost no young men in the community. Roughly half of the families had sons, brothers or husbands in the Communist ranks. The remaining families were about equally divided between those with neutral attitudes and those who were Government sympathizers.

The morning after I arrived, the peasants, under the supervision of the Government pacification workers, began constructing a fence around the hamlet perimeter to keep out Vietcong infiltrators. Through an interpreter, I asked two farmers among a group of old men, women and children digging postholes if they thought the fence would be of any use.

"Maybe it will," one said, "but I don't think so. A fence won't keep out the Vietcong."

"What did the Vietcong make you do when they controlled the hamlet?" I asked.

---

[7] cannon fodder—food for cannons—that is, those who are killed by both sides.

"They made us pull down the fence we had put up before, and dig trenches and lay booby traps," the second farmer said.

"Well, if you don't think the fence will do any good," I asked, "why are you putting it up?"

"We are just plain farmers," the first peasant said, glancing apprehensively at a policeman a few feet away with a carbine slung across his arm. "We have to obey any Government here."

As he spoke, a Vietcong sniper, hidden in a patch of sugar cane beyond the paddy fields, fired two shots. The old men, women and children scurried for cover, their fear and lack of enthusiasm for fence-building evident on their faces.

During a tour of South Vietnam in 1963, Gen. Earle G.Wheeler, chairman of the Joint Chiefs of Staff, referred to the conflict as a "dirty little war." While the Vietnam conflict may be even dirtier now than it was in 1963, it can no longer be termed little.

Reliable statistics are very elusive in Vietnam, but I would estimate that at least 250,000 persons have been killed since the war began in 1957. Last year, according to official figures, 34,585 Communists were killed and the Saigon Government forces suffered 11,200 deaths. Through mid-September of this year, again according to official statistics, 37,299 Vietcong and North Vietnamese regulars have died in battle and 7,017 Government troops have been killed.

American losses remained at a relatively low level until 1965, when the Johnson Administration committed ground combat units and began to create an expeditionary corps. That year, 1,369 American servicemen died in North and South Vietnam and neighboring Laos, and 6,114 were wounded. This year, as American offensive operations have picked up stride with the strengthening of the logistical apparatus, casualties have soared to 3,524 killed and 21,107 wounded, through mid-September. American dead are now averaging nearly a hundred a week and can be expected to increase as the expeditionary corps grows and more Americans are exposed to hostile fire.

The attitudes of the leadership in Hanoi and Washington indicate that the contest is far from being resolved. The rate at which North Vietnam is infiltrating its regular troops into the South and the willingness of the United States to engage its own ground forces and to escalate the air war against the North portend[8] several more years of serious bloodshed. The world may hope for peace, but neither side has yet hurt the other sufficiently to prevent it from continuing. Both sides are trapped in a dilemma created by their history and political and strategic considerations. Washington cannot withdraw its troops from South Vietnam, as Hanoi demands, without making certain an eventual Communist seizure of power there and negating all the efforts of the last decade to maintain a friendly Government in Saigon.

Hanoi's best chance of winning now lies in prolonging the bloodletting to the point where the American public will tire of a war for a small land whose name most Americans cannot even pronounce correctly (they tend to say "Veetnam"). If the North de-escalates the fighting it will remove the principal source of political pressure on the Johnson Administration—the number of coffins being flown home from Saigon. Without the killing, the United States might be able to occupy South Vietnam indefinitely. The fact that 60,000 U.S. troops are stationed in South Korea brings no demonstrators into the streets and arouses no anxiety among American mothers, because the shooting in Korea has stopped.

A year ago, I worried that the patience of the American people would run out, that Ho Chi Minh would have his way and that the United States would

---

[8] portend—give an omen or sign.

lose the Vietnam war. This fear no longer troubles me nearly as much. I have the feeling that somehow we can muddle through this grim business. We may not win in Vietnam as we won in World War II, yet we may well prevail. Given our overwhelming military superiority, it is entirely possible that Washington, over a period of years, may be able to destroy the Vietcong and North Vietnamese main-force units in the South, and to transform what is currently a militarily sound but politically weak position into one of some, if doubtful, political strength.

Rather, my quiet worry concerns what we are doing to ourselves in the course of prosecuting and possibly some day winning this war. In World War II and in Korea the aggression of one state against another was an established fact. The United States acted with clear moral justification and Americans fought as they always like to think they fight—for human freedom and dignity. In Vietnam this moral superiority has given way to the amorality of great power politics, specifically, to the problem of maintaining the United States as the paramount power in Southeast Asia. The Vietnamese people have become mere pawns in the struggle. Whatever desires they might possess have become incidental. The United States can no longer make any pretense of fighting to safeguard South Vietnam's independence. The presence of 317,000 American troops in the country has made a mockery of its sovereignty and the military junta[9] in Saigon would not last a week without American bayonets to protect it.

Precisely because the Saigon Government represents nothing beyond its administration and army, the United States has had to fall back on its own military force to maintain its position and to win the war. Washington can dispense the latest in weaponry, but

---

[9] junta—a group of military officers ruling a country after seizing power.

the First Air Cavalry Division and the Third Marine Amphibious Force cannot inspire the loyalty of the Vietnamese peasantry, and General Motors cannot manufacture decent non-Communist Vietnamese leadership, effective government and dedication. Only Vietnamese can supply these and the non-Communist Vietnamese have proven themselves incapable of providing them.

Thus, in the final analysis, American strategy in Vietnam consists of creating a killing machine in the form of a highly equipped expeditionary corps and then turning this machine on the enemy in the hope that over the years enough killing will be done to force the enemy's collapse through exhaustion and despair. This strategy, although possibly the only feasible alternative open to a modern industrial power in such a situation, is of necessity brutal and heedless of many of its victims.

Despite these misgivings, I do not see how we can do anything but continue to prosecute the war. We can and should limit the violence and the suffering being inflicted on the civilians as much as possible, but for whatever reasons, successive Administrations in Washington have carried the commitment in Vietnam to the point where it would be very difficult to prevent any precipitate retreat from degenerating into a **rout**.[10] If the United States were to disengage from Vietnam under adverse conditions, I believe that the resulting political and psychological shockwaves might undermine our entire position in Southeast Asia. We shall, I am afraid, have to put up with our Vietnamese **mandarin**[11] allies. We shall not be able to reform them and it is unlikely that we shall be able to

---

[10] **rout**—state of wild confusion.

[11] **mandarin**—Chinese person of position and influence.

find any other Vietnamese willing to cooperate with us. We shall have to continue to rely mainly on our military power, accept the **odium**[12] attached to its use and hope that someday this power will bring us to a favorable settlement.

But I simply cannot help worrying that, in the process of waging this war, we are corrupting ourselves. I wonder, when I look at the bombed-out peasant hamlets, the orphans begging and stealing on the streets of Saigon and the women and children with napalm burns lying on the hospital cots, whether the United States or any nation has the right to inflict this suffering and degradation on another people for its own ends. And I hope we will not, in the name of some anti-Communist crusade, do this again.

---

[12] **odium**—disgrace.

QUESTIONS TO CONSIDER

1. How does Neil Sheehan's attitude toward the Vietnam War change over time?

2. Why have the Vietnamese peasants left their homes in record numbers?

3. What are some of the "maladies" America introduced to Vietnam?

4. What does Sheehan propose the U.S. should do in Vietnam? Explain in your own words.

from

America's Longest War

BY GEORGE C. HERRING

At the end of 1967, the head of U.S. military operations in Vietnam,
William Westmoreland, flew to the U.S. and spoke before Congress
about U.S. military successes and a forthcoming victory. But on
January 31, North Vietnamese and Viet Cong forces launched a
massive assault against U.S. positions. All of the major cities of
South Vietnam were attacked, including the capital, Saigon. In a
daring raid, Viet Cong guerrillas attacked the American embassy in
Saigon and held it under siege for five hours. This offensive began
during the traditional Tet holiday when many South Vietnamese
troops were on leave. The goal of the offensive was to start a popular
uprising and cause South Vietnamese units to defect or fall apart.
It failed in both these goals, and U.S. forces were able to retake
all of the lost positions, often inflicting heavy casualties on the
Viet Cong and North Vietnamese. However, the offensive is now
generally thought to have been the turning point in the war. Tet
was the beginning of the end of U.S. commitments in Vietnam.

At 2:45 A.M. on January 30, 1968, a team of Vietcong sappers[1] blasted a large hole in the wall surrounding the United States Embassy in Saigon and dashed into the courtyard of the compound. For the next six hours, the most important symbol of the American presence in Vietnam was the scene of one of the most dramatic episodes of the war. Unable to get through the heavy door at the main entrance of the Embassy building, the attackers retreated to the courtyard and took cover behind large concrete flower pots, pounding the building with rockets and exchanging gunfire with a small detachment of military police. They held their positions until 9:15 A.M., when they were finally over-powered. All nineteen of the Vietcong were killed or severely wounded.

The attack on the Embassy was but a small part of the Tet Offensive, a massive, coordinated Vietcong assault against the major urban areas of South Vietnam. In most other locales, the result was the same: the attackers were repulsed and incurred heavy losses. Later that morning, standing in the Embassy courtyard amidst the debris and fallen bodies in a scene one reporter described as a "butcher shop in Eden," Westmoreland[2] rendered his initial assessment of Tet. The "well-laid plans" of the North Vietnamese and Vietcong had failed, he observed. "The enemy exposed himself by virtue of his strategy and he suffered heavy casualties." Although his comments brought moans of disbelief from the assembled journalists, from a short-term tactical standpoint Westmoreland was correct: Tet represented a defeat for the enemy. As Bernard Brodie has observed, however, the Tet Offensive was "probably unique in that the side that lost completely in the tactical sense came away with

---

[1] sappers—military engineers who lay, detect, and disarm mines.

[2] Westmoreland—The American general William Westmoreland (1914–) commanded U.S. forces in South Vietnam in the Vietnam War from 1964 to 1968.

an overwhelming psychological and hence political victory." Tet had a tremendous impact in the United States and ushered in a new phase of a seemingly endless war.

In the spring or summer of 1967, the North Vietnamese decided upon a change in strategy. Some Americans have depicted the Tet Offensive as a last-gasp, desperation move, comparable to the Battle of the Bulge, in which a beleaguered North Vietnam attempted to snatch victory from the jaws of defeat. This seems quite doubtful although Hanoi's decision to take the offensive probably did reflect growing concern with the heavy casualties in the south and fear of the costs of a prolonged war of attrition with the United States. It seems more likely that the offensive was born of excessive optimism, a growing perception that the urban areas of South Vietnam were ripe for revolution. There are no indications that Hanoi thought the offensive would be decisive, however. Certainly its leaders would have been pleased to force the collapse of the South Vietnamese government and bring about an American withdrawal. Most probably, they viewed the offensive as an essential part of a complex, multifaceted, long-term strategy of "fighting while negotiating." There is no evidence that the North Vietnamese timed the offensive to coincide with the first stages of the American presidential election campaign, although they certainly hoped to exploit the rising discontent with the war in the United States.

Sometime in 1967, Hanoi began developing specific plans to implement the new strategy. To lure American troops away from the major population centers and maintain a high level of U.S. casualties, a series of large-scale diversionary attacks were to be launched in remote areas. These would be followed by coordinated Vietcong assaults against the major cities and towns of South Vietnam designed to weaken the government and ignite a "general uprising" among the population.

Simultaneously, new efforts would be made to open negotiations with the United States. The North Vietnamese most probably hoped through these coordinated actions to get the bombing stopped, weaken the Saigon regime, **exacerbate**[3] differences between the United States and its South Vietnamese ally, and intensify pressures for a change in policy in the United States. Their ultimate objective was to secure an acceptable negotiated settlement, the minimum ingredients of which would have been a coalition government and a U.S. withdrawal.

Hanoi began executing its plan in late 1967. In October and November, North Vietnamese regulars attacked the Marine base at Con Thien across the Laotian border, and the towns of Loc Ninh and Song Be near Saigon and Dak To in the Central Highlands. Shortly after, two North Vietnamese divisions laid siege to the Marine garrison at Khe Sanh near the Laotian border. In the meantime, crack Vietcong units moved into the cities and towns, accumulating supplies and laying final plans. To undermine the Saigon government, the National Liberation Front encouraged the formation of a "popular front" of neutralists, and attempted to **entice**[4] government officials and troops to defect by offering generous pardons and positions in a coalition government. To spread dissension between the United States and Thieu, the front opened secret contacts with the American Embassy in Saigon and disseminated rumors of peace talks. Hanoi followed in December 1967 by stating categorically that it would negotiate with the United States if Johnson stopped the bombing.

The first phase of the North Vietnamese plan worked to perfection. Westmoreland quickly dispatched reinforcements to Con Thien, Loc Ninh, Song Be, and Dak To, in each case driving back the North Vietnamese and

---

[3] **exacerbate**—make more severe.

[4] **entice**—to attract by arousing hope or desire; lure.

inflicting heavy losses but dispersing U.S. forces and leaving the cities vulnerable. By the end of 1967, moreover, the attention of Westmoreland, the President, and indeed much of the nation, was riveted on Khe Sanh, which many Americans assumed was Giap's play for a repetition of Dienbienphu.[5] The press and television carried daily reports of the action. Johnson, insisting that the fortress must be held at all costs, kept close watch on the battle with a terrain map in the White House "war room." Westmoreland sent 6,000 men to defend the garrison, and American B-52s carried out the heaviest air raids in the history of warfare, eventually dropping more than 100,000 tons of explosives on a five-square-mile battlefield.

While the United States was preoccupied with Khe Sanh, the North Vietnamese and Vietcong prepared for the second phase of the operation. The offensive against the cities was timed to coincide with the beginning of Tet, the lunar new year and the most festive of Vietnamese holidays. Throughout the war, both sides had traditionally observed a cease-fire during Tet, and Hanoi correctly assumed that South Vietnam would be relaxing and celebrating, soldiers visiting their families, government officials away from their offices. While the Americans and South Vietnamese prepared for the holidays, Vietcong units readied themselves for the bloodiest battles of the war. Mingling with the heavy holiday traffic, guerrillas disguised as ARVN soldiers or civilians moved into the cities and towns, some audaciously hitching rides on American vehicles. Weapons were smuggled in on vegetable carts and even in mock funeral processions.

---

[5] Dienbienphu—In the Battle of Dien Bien Phu (1954), Vietnamese insurgents surrounded the French-controlled village of Dien Bien Phu. The battle, which lasted from March 13 to May 7, resulted in French casualties of more than 15,000 troops. France's defeat at Dien Bien Phu led to the Geneva agreements of July 21, 1954, which arranged for a cease-fire and the end of French colonial rule of Vietnam, Laos, and Cambodia.

Within twenty-four hours after the beginning of Tet, January 30, 1968, the Vietcong launched a series of attacks extending from the demilitarized zone to the Ca Mau Peninsula on the southern tip of Vietnam. In all, they struck thirty-six of forty-four provincial capitals, five of the six major cities, sixty-four district capitals, and fifty hamlets. In addition to the daring raid on the Embassy, Vietcong units assaulted Saigon's Tan Son Nhut Airport, the presidential palace, and the headquarters of South Vietnam's general staff. In Hue, 7,500 Vietcong and North Vietnamese troops stormed and eventually took control of the ancient Citadel, the interior town which had been the seat of the Emperors of the Kingdom of Annam.

The offensive caught the United States and South Vietnam off guard. American intelligence had picked up signs of intensive Vietcong activity in and around the cities and had even translated captured documents which, without giving dates, outlined the plan in some detail. The U.S. command was so preoccupied with Khe Sanh, however, that it viewed evidence pointing to the cities as a diversion to distract it from the main battlefield. As had happened so often before, the United States underestimated the capability of the enemy. The North Vietnamese appeared so bloodied by the campaigns of 1967 that the Americans could not conceive that they could bounce back and deliver a blow of the magnitude of Tet. "Even had I known exactly what was to take place," Westmoreland's intelligence officer later conceded, "it was so preposterous that I probably would have been unable to sell it to anybody."

Although taken by surprise, the United States and South Vietnam recovered quickly. The timing of the offensive was poorly coordinated, and premature attacks in some towns sounded a warning which enabled Westmoreland to get reinforcements to vulnerable areas. In addition, the Vietcong was slow to capitalize on its initial successes, giving the United States time to mount a strong defense. In Saigon, American and ARVN forces held off the initial attacks and within several days had cleared the city, inflicting huge casualties, taking large numbers of prisoners, and forcing the remnants to melt into the countryside. Elsewhere the result was much the same. The ARVN fought better under pressure than any American would have dared predict, and the United States and South Vietnam used their superior mobility and firepower to devastating advantage. The Vietcong launched a second round of attacks on February 18, but these were confined largely to rocket and mortar barrages against U.S. and South Vietnamese military installations and steadily diminished in intensity.

Hue was the only exception to the general pattern. The liberation of that city took nearly three weeks, required heavy bombing and intensive artillery fire, and ranks among the bloodiest and most destructive battles of the war. The United States and South Vietnam lost an estimated 500 killed while enemy killed in action have been estimated as high as 5,000. The savage fighting caused huge numbers of civilian casualties and created an estimated 100,000 refugees. The bodies of 2,800 South Vietnamese were found in mass graves in and around Hue, the product of Vietcong and North Vietnamese executions, and another 2,000 citizens of Hue were unaccounted for and presumed murdered. The beautiful city, with its many architectural treasures, was left, in the words of one observer, a "shattered, stinking hulk, its streets choked with rubble and rotting bodies."

It remains difficult to assess the impact of the battles of Tet. The North Vietnamese and Vietcong did not force the collapse of South Vietnam. They were unable to establish any firm positions in the urban areas, and the South Vietnamese people did not rise up to welcome them as "liberators." Vietcong and North Vietnamese battle deaths have been estimated as high as 40,000, and although this figure may be inflated, the losses were huge. The Vietcong bore the brunt of the fighting; its regular units were decimated and would never completely recover, and its political infrastructure suffered crippling losses.

If, in these terms, Tet represented a "defeat" for the enemy, it was still a costly "victory" for the United States and South Vietnam. ARVN forces had to be withdrawn from the countryside to defend the cities, and the pacification program incurred another major setback. The destruction visited upon the cities heaped formidable new problems on a government that had shown limited capacity to deal with the routine. American and South Vietnamese losses did not approach those of the enemy, but they were still high: in the first two weeks of the Tet campaigns, the United States lost 1,100 killed in action and South Vietnam 2,300. An estimated 12,500 civilians were killed, and Tet created as many as one million new refugees. As with much of the war, there was a great deal of destruction and suffering, but no clearcut winner or loser.

To the extent that the North Vietnamese designed the Tet Offensive to influence the United States, they succeeded, for it sent instant shock waves across the nation. Early wire service reports exaggerated the success of the raid on the Embassy, some even indicating that the Vietcong had occupied several floors of the building. Although these initial reports were in time corrected, the reaction was still one of disbelief. "What the hell is going on?" the venerable newscaster Walter Cronkite is said to have snapped. "I thought we were winning the war!" Televised accounts of the bloody fighting in Saigon and Hue made a mockery of Johnson and of Westmoreland's optimistic year-end reports, widening the credibility gap, and cynical journalists openly mocked Westmoreland's claims of victory. The humorist Art Buchwald parodied the general's statements in terms of Custer at Little Big Horn. "We have the Sioux on the run," Buchwald had Custer saying. "Of course we still have some cleaning up to do, but the Redskins are hurting badly and it will only be a matter of time before they give in." The battles of Tet raised to a new level of public consciousness basic questions about the war which had long lurked just beneath the surface. The offhand remark of a U.S. Army officer who had participated in the liberation of the delta village of Ben Tre—"We had to destroy the town to save it"— seemed to **epitomize**[6] the purposeless destruction of the war. Candid photographs of the police chief of Saigon holding a pistol to the head of a Vietcong captive—and then firing—starkly symbolized the way in which violence had triumphed over morality and law.

---

[6] **epitomize**—to be a typical example of.

QUESTIONS TO CONSIDER

1. What was the American public's reaction to the Tet Offensive?

2. What were the two phases of the Tet Offensive?

3. Why was the U.S. government so surprised by the Tet Offensive?

"We Are Mired in Stalemate..."

BY WALTER CRONKITE

*Vietnam is sometimes known as the "living room war" because television crews and reporters brought home every detail to the American public. There are many **indelible**[1] images of Vietnam: scenes such as a monk **immolating**[2] himself in Saigon, bodies dumped in a trench at My Lai, and a South Vietnamese girl hit by napalm running down a street. These images shaped public opinion in a way that the sanitized and censored images and reports from WWII and the Korean War did not. They made it personal for many Americans. In the wake of the Tet Offensive, the nightly news played a key role in defining the "credibility gap": the difference between reality and what the government was saying was occurring in Vietnam. One of the most important events in opinion-shaping was an editorial delivered by CBS anchorman Walter Cronkite in February 1968. Afterward, President Johnson commented to his aides that "If I've lost Walter, then it's over." Below is the text of Cronkite's television editorial of February 27, 1968.*

---

[1] **indelible**—impossible to remove, erase, or wash away; permanent.

[2] **immolating**—killing oneself as a sacrifice.

Tonight, back in more familiar surroundings in New York, we'd like to sum up our findings in Vietnam, an analysis that must be speculative, personal, subjective. Who won and who lost in the great Tet offensive against the cities? I'm not sure. The Vietcong did not win by a knockout, but neither did we. The referees of history may make it a draw. Another standoff may be coming in the big battles expected south of the Demilitarized Zone. Khe Sanh could well fall, with a terrible loss in American lives, prestige and morale, and this is a tragedy of our stubbornness there; but the bastion no longer is a key to the rest of the northern regions, and it is doubtful that the American forces can be defeated across the breadth of the D M Z with any substantial loss of ground. Another standoff. On the political front, past performance gives no confidence that the Vietnamese government can cope with its problems, now compounded by the attack on the cities. It may not fall, it may hold on, but it probably won't show the dynamic qualities demanded of this young nation. Another standoff.

We have been too often disappointed by the optimism of the American leaders, both in Vietnam and Washington, to have faith any longer in the silver linings they find in the darkest clouds. They may be right, that Hanoi's winter-spring offensive has been forced by the Communist realization that they could not win the longer war of attrition, and that the Communists hope that any success in the offensive will improve their position for eventual negotiations. It would improve their position, and it would also require our realization, that we should have had all along, that any negotiations must be that—negotiations, not the dictation of peace terms. For it seems now more certain than ever that the bloody experience of Vietnam is to end in a **stalemate**.[3] This summer's almost certain standoff will either end in real give-and-take negotiations or terrible escalation;

---

[3] **stalemate**—a situation in which further action is blocked; a deadlock.

and for every means we have to escalate, the enemy can match us, and that applies to invasion of the North, the use of nuclear weapons, or the mere commitment of one hundred, or two hundred, or three hundred thousand more American troops to the battle. And with each escalation, the world comes closer to the brink of cosmic disaster.

To say that we are closer to victory today is to believe, in the face of the evidence, the optimists who have been wrong in the past. To suggest we are on the edge of defeat is to yield to unreasonable pessimism. To say that we are **mired**[4] in stalemate seems the only realistic, yet unsatisfactory, conclusion. On the off chance that military and political analysts are right, in the next few months we must test the enemy's intentions, in case this is indeed his last big gasp before negotiations. But it is increasingly clear to this reporter that the only rational way out then will be to negotiate, not as victors, but as an honorable people who lived up to their pledge to defend democracy, and did the best they could.

This is Walter Cronkite. Good night.

---

[4] **mired**—sunk or stuck.

QUESTIONS TO CONSIDER

1. What is the "credibility gap"?

2. How does Cronkite support his prediction that the war will end in stalemate?

3. What does Cronkite think the U.S. should do about Vietnam?

My Lai Massacre

BY SEYMOUR HERSH

*On March 16, 1968, a platoon led by Lt. William Calley was sent to secure the village of My Lai, termed Pinkville and suspected of being a Viet Cong **stronghold**.[1] In the course of this operation, Calley and his men systematically murdered 347 Vietnamese civilians, including many women and children. This massacre was willfully **perpetrated**[2] over a series of hours and is one of the most horrific events of the war. Calley ordered his men to shoot and keep killing. The army successfully covered up the massacre until 1969, when reports by the journalist Seymour Hersh brought the atrocities to light. Lt. Calley and four others were court-martialed,[3] but only Calley was sent to jail. The incident only increased the American public's already substantial disillusionment with the war in Vietnam.*

---

[1] **stronghold**—an area dominated or occupied by a special group.

[2] **perpetrated**—committed.

[3] court-martialed—prosecuted by a military or naval court of law.

TERRE HAUTE, Ind., NOV. 25—A former GI told in interviews yesterday how he executed, under orders, dozens of South Vietnamese civilians during the United States Army attack on the village of Song My in March 1968. He estimated that he and his fellow soldiers shot 370 villagers during the operation in what has become known as Pinkville.

Paul Meadlo, 22 years old, West Terre Haute, Ind., a farm community near the Illinois border, gave an eye-witness account—the first made available thus far—of what happened when a platoon led by Lt. William L. Calley, Jr. entered Pinkville on a search-and-destroy mission. The Army has acknowledged that at least 100 civilians were killed by the men; Vietnamese survivors had told reporters that the death total was 567.

Meadlo, who was wounded in a mine accident the day after Pinkville, disclosed that the company captain, Ernest Medina, was in the area at the time of the shootings and made no attempt to stop them.

Calley, 26, Waynesville, N.C., has been accused of the premeditated murder of 109 civilians in the incident. Medina, as commander of the Eleventh Infantry Brigade unit, is under investigation for his role in the shootings. Last week the Army said that at least 24 other men were under investigation, including Calley's chief noncommissioned[4] officer, Sgt. David Mitchell, 29, St. Francisville, La., who is being investigated for assault with intent to commit murder. Calley was ordered yesterday to stand general court-martial.

Here is Meadlo's story as given in interviews at his mother's home near Terre Haute:

"There was supposed to have been some Viet Cong in Pinkville and we began to make a sweep through it. Once we got there we began gathering up the people . . .

---

[4] noncommissioned—an enlisted member of the armed forces, such as a corporal, sergeant, or petty officer, appointed to a rank conferring leadership over other enlisted personnel.

started putting them in big mobs. There must have been about 40 or 45 civilians standing in one big circle in the middle of the village . . . Calley told me and a couple of other guys to watch them.

"'You know what I want you to do with them' he said," Meadlo related. He and the others continued to guard the group. "About 10 minutes later Calley came back. 'Get with it,' he said. 'I want them dead.'

"So we stood about 10 or 15 feet away from them, then he (Calley) started shooting them. Then he told me to start shooting them. . . . I started to shoot them, but the other guys (who had been assigned to guard the civilians) wouldn't do it.

"So we (Meadlo and Calley) went ahead and killed them. I used more than a whole clip—actually I used four or five clips," Meadlo said. (There are 17 M-16 shells in a clip.) He estimated that he killed at least 15 civilians—or nearly half of those in the circle.

Asked what he thought at the time, Meadlo said, "I just thought we were supposed to do it." Later, he said that the shooting "did take a load off my conscience for the buddies we'd lost. It was just revenge, that's all it was."

The company had been in the field for 40 days without relief before the Pinkville incident on March 16, and had lost a number of men in mine accidents. Hostility to the Vietnamese was high in the company, Meadlo said.

The killings continued.

"We had about seven or eight civilians gathered in a hootch,[5] and I was going to throw a hand grenade in. But someone told us to take them to the ditch (a drainage ditch in the village into which many civilians were herded—and shot).

"Calley was there and said to me, 'Meadlo, we've got another job to do.' So we pushed our seven to eight

---

[5] hootch—slang for a Vietnamese house or hut.

people in with the big bunch of them. And so I began shooting them all. So did Mitchell, Calley . . . (At this point Meadlo could not remember any more men involved). I guess I shot maybe 25 or 20 people in the ditch."

His role in the killings had not yet ended.

"After the ditch, there were just some people in hootches. I knew there were some people down in one hootch, maybe two or three, so I just threw a hand grenade in."

Meadlo is a tall, clean-cut son of an Indiana coal mine worker. He married his high-school sweetheart in suburban Terre Haute, began rearing a family (he has two children) and was drafted. He had been in Vietnam four months at the time of Pinkville. On the next day, March 17, his foot was blown off, when, while following Calley on an operation, a land mine was set off.

As Meadlo was waiting to be evacuated, other men in the company had reported that he told Calley that "this was his (Meadlo's) punishment for what he had done the day before." He warned, according to onlookers, that Calley would have his day of judgment too. Asked about this, Meadlo said he could not remember.

Meadlo is back at a factory job now in Terre Haute, fighting to keep a full disability payment from the Veterans' Administration. The loss of his right foot seems to bother him less than the loss of his self-respect.

Like other members of his company, he had been called just days before the interview by an officer at Fort Benning, Ga., where Calley is being held, and advised that he should not discuss the case with reporters. But, like other members of his company, he seemed eager to talk.

"This has made him awful nervous," explained his mother, Mrs. Myrtle Meadlo, 57, New Goshen, Ind. "He seems like he just can't get over it.

"I sent them a good boy and they made him a murderer."

Why did he do it?

"We all were under orders," Meadlo said. "We all thought we were doing the right thing. . . . At the time it didn't bother me."

He began having serious doubts that night about what he had done at Pinkville. He says he still has them.

"The kids and the women—they didn't have any right to die.

"In the beginning," Meadlo said, "I just thought we were going to be murdering the Viet Cong." He, like other members of his company, had attended a squad meeting the night before, at which time Company Commander Medina promised the boys a good firefight.

Calley and his platoon were assigned the key role of entering the Pinkville area first.

"When we came in we thought we were getting fired on," Meadlo said, although the company suffered no casualties, apparently because the Viet Cong had fled from the area during the night.

"We came in from this open field, and somebody spotted this one gook[6] out there. He was down in a shelter, scared and huddling. . . . Someone said, 'There's a gook over here,' and asked what to do with him. Mitchell said, 'Shoot him,' and he did. The gook was standing up and shaking and waving his arms when he got it.

"Then we came onto this hootch, and one door was hard to open."

Meadlo said he crashed through the door and "found an old man in there shaking."

"I told them, 'I got one,' and it was Mitchell who told me to shoot him. That was the first man I shot. He

---

[6] gook—a derogatory term used during the war to refer to a person of Vietnamese descent.

was hiding in a dugout, shaking his head and waving his arms, trying to tell me not to shoot him."

After the carnage, Meadlo said, "I heard that all we were supposed to do was kill the V C. Mitchell said we were just supposed to shoot the men."

Women and children also were shot. Meadlo estimated that at least 310 persons were shot to death by the Americans that day.

"I know it was far more than 100 as the U.S. Army now says. I'm absolutely sure of that. There were bodies all around."

He has some haunting memories, he says. "They didn't put up a fight or anything. The women huddled against their children and took it. They brought their kids real close to their stomachs and hugged them, and put their bodies over them trying to save them. It didn't do much good," Meadlo said.

Two things puzzled him. He vigorously disputes the repeated reports of an artillery barrage before the village was approached.

"There wasn't any artillery barrage whatsoever in the village. Only some gunships firing from above," he said.

The South Vietnamese government said Saturday that 20 civilians were killed in the Pinkville attack, most of them victims of tactical air strikes or an artillery barrage laid down before the U.S. troops moved in. The government denied reports of a massacre.

Meadlo is curious also about the role of Capt. Medina in the incident.

"I don't know if the C.O. (Company Commander) gave the order to kill or not, but he was right there when it happened. Why didn't he stop it? He and Calley passed each other quite a few times that morning, but didn't say anything. Medina just kept marching around. He could've put a stop to it anytime he wanted."

The whole operation took about 30 minutes, Meadlo said.

As for Calley, Meadlo told of an incident a few weeks before Pinkville.

"We saw this woman walking across this rice paddy and Calley said, 'Shoot her,' so we did. When we got there the girl was alive, had this hole in her side. Calley tried to get someone to shoot her again; I don't know if he did."

In addition, Calley and Medina had told the men before Pinkville, Meadlo said, "that if we ever shoot any civilians, we should go ahead and plant a hand grenade on them."

Meadlo is not sure, but he thinks the feel of death came quickly to the company once it got to Vietnam.

"We were cautious at first, but as soon as the first man was killed, a new feeling came through the company . . . almost as if we all knew there was going to be a lot more killing."

QUESTIONS TO CONSIDER

1. What does Mrs. Meadlo mean when she says, "I sent them a good boy and they made him a murderer"?

2. Why do you think prompted Calley and Medina to order the massacre?

3. Why do you think Paul Meadlo agrees to participate, even though some of the other soldiers refuse?

from

Bloods

BY WALLACE TERRY

Joseph Anderson was a young lieutenant, a recent graduate of the U.S. military academy at West Point, when he was sent to Vietnam in command of a battalion. Anderson quickly made a name for himself and his unit of the First Cavalry division. Anderson was one of the few African-American officers out of West Point and in command of a unit of mixed races. In 1966, the United States still had serious racial divides, but in the army at war soldiers of all races quickly became comrades. As another soldier, Robert Sanders, wrote: "Sometimes it takes a tragedy to bring people together. It really does. And I can't think of anything more tragic than that situation at the time. Little things happened. Guys ran out of cigarettes; they shared." Anderson's account of his time in Vietnam is taken from Bloods, *Wallace Terry's oral history of the African-American experience in Vietnam.*

Captain Joseph B. Anderson, Jr.:

Shortly after I got to Vietnam, we got into a real big fight. We were outnumbered at least ten to one. But I didn't know it.

I had taken over 1st Platoon of B Company of the 1st of the 12th Cav. We were up against a Viet Cong battalion. There may have been 300 to 400 of them.

And they had just wiped out one of our platoons. At that time in the war, summer of 1966, it was a terrible loss. A bloody massacre.

This platoon had been dropped in a landing zone called LZ Pink in the Central Highlands to do a search and destroy operation. It was probably eight o'clock in the morning. They didn't realize that they were surrounded. After the helicopters left, the V C opened up and just wiped 'em out. They knocked out the radios, too, so nobody knew what happened to them.

My platoon happened to be out on patrol some miles away. We were the closest to the area of their intended operation. So when there was no word from them, I was given instructions to move in the direction of where they had been dropped and try to find where they had gone.

This is my first operation. I'm new in country. People don't know me. I don't know them. They have to be thinking, Can this platoon leader handle it? I was only a second lieutenant.

We went into a forced march all day. When it got dark, we pulled into a clear area like a landing zone and put our perimeter out and set up for the night. Headquarters wanted me to keep moving and keep searching through the night. I knew it wasn't a smart thing to do, because you could get ambushed. You can't see what you're doing in the dark.

Around ten or eleven o'clock, they opened up on us. They were still there. We fought all night long, until six in the morning.

I learned very quickly how to call in artillery, how to put aircraft over me to drop flares and keep the area lighted up so they couldn't sneak up on me.

I was calling the artillery in within 35, 40 yards of my own people, as tight as I could without hitting us.

I can't remember wondering if I was ever gonna get out of this. I just did not have time to think about it. I was just too busy directing fire to be scared.

After we drove them off, we began to fan out and search the area. We found the ambushed platoon just 50 yards away. About 25 of them were dead. There were four still alive, but badly wounded. They must have played dead, because all the bodies had been searched and stripped of weapons and equipment. Then four more members of that platoon who had gotten away came out of the jungle to join us. Only one of my men had been hurt. He was shot in the hip.

For rescuing the survivors and driving off the VC battalion I received a Silver Star. But most importantly, the action served as a bond between my platoon and me. It was my first chance to react under fire, and it had gone well. My men knew I could handle the responsibility.

I was an absolute rarity in Vietnam. A black West Pointer commanding troops. One year after graduation. I was very aggressive about my role and responsibilities as an Army officer serving in Vietnam. I was there to defend the freedom of the South Vietnamese government, stabilize the countryside, and help contain communism. The Domino Theory[1] was dominant then, predominant as a matter of fact. I was gung ho. And I thought the war would last three years at the most.

There weren't many opportunities for blacks in private industry then. And as a graduate of West

[1] Domino Theory—theory coined by President Dwight Eisenhower that the fall of one country to Communism would lead eventually to the fall of neighboring countries.

Point, I was an officer and a gentleman by act of Congress. Where else could a black go and get that label just like that?

Throughout the Cav, the black representation in the enlisted ranks was heavier than the population as a whole in the United States. One third of my platoon and two of my four squad leaders were black. For many black men, the service, even during a war, was the best of a number of alternatives to staying home and working in the fields or bumming around the streets of Chicago or New York.

Earlier that year, French National Television hired Pierre Schoendoerffer to produce a film about America's participation in the war. He had been with the French forces at the fall of Dien Bien Phu to the Communist forces in North Vietnam. After visiting different operations around the country, both Army and Marine, he settled on the 1st Cav because of the new approach of our air mobility, our helicopter orientation. And he wound up with my platoon because of its racial mix— we had American Indians and Mexican-Americans, too—our success in finding the lost platoon, my West Point background and ability to speak French. He and the film crew stayed with us day and night for six weeks, filming everything we did. They spoke very good English, and I didn't speak good enough French. And Schoendoerffer had as much knowledge and experience about the war as any of us.

The film would be called *The Anderson Platoon*. And it would make us famous.

During the filming in late September, we encountered another Viet Cong battalion in a village right on the edge of the coast. A couple of scout helicopters had been patrolling, looking for enemy signs. The Viet Cong fired on them and shot them down. We were already lifted off that morning, going to another location, when we were diverted to the scene. In air mobility. The basic concept of the 1st Cavalry Division. And it worked.

My platoon was the first one on the ground. We blocked a northern route of **egress,**[2] and then we started to sweep south through the village. It's amazing. We walked through the village, through their entire battalion, to link up with our company on the other side. And they never fired a shot. To this day I don't know why.

Meanwhile, the division piled on. We put about a brigade in, three battalions, and surrounded the village about a mile across. We did it so quick, they were fixed. They couldn't escape. And with artillery, aircraft, and naval gunfire off the coast, we really waged a high-powered conflict. But not without casualties.

Around noon, my platoon sergeant, a white guy named Watson from Missouri, and some of his people were searching holes in the ground, and they threw a grenade in to see if any enemy were in it. The enemy was in there and threw the grenade back out, wounding Watson and three others. We had to pull back to get them out on a medevac.

I made Owens the platoon sergeant. He was a black guy from California who was as professional as they come.

Around four o'clock, another platoon got in trouble, and we started moving to help them. Owens's squad moved on the attack first, then he got hit in the head, a bullet crease. And we had to consolidate our position and medevac him out.

I remember very distinctly chastising my organization for firing during that night. I felt they were spooked and just shooting at shadows. The next morning, there were all kinds of bodies out there, where the Viet Cong were trying to slip out to escape the encirclement.

---

[2] **egress**—the act of coming or going out; emergence.

That was one lopsided operation. We lost only four or five men, maybe thirty wounded. But the Viet Cong lost more than 200 killed. . . .

Career officers and enlisted men like me did not go back to a hostile environment in America. We went back to bases where we were assimilated and congratulated and decorated for our performance in the conduct of the war.

The others were rejected, because the nation experienced a defeat. The nation heard stories of atrocities, of drugs. Everyone who was in Vietnam was suspect. And that generalization is unfair to apply to all the people who were there. In two tours I just did not experience any atrocities. Sure, you shot to kill. But personally I did not experience cutting off ears from dead bodies or torturing captured prisoners.

Long before Saigon fell, it was clear to me the United States was not willing to win the war. So the only alternative is to lose the war.

When Saigon did fall, the only feeling I had was, you might expect that considering how things deteriorated. There was no remorse, no feeling of life wasted.

I was at peace with myself about my behavior and my contribution to the process. I went over there and I did what I had to do. I didn't volunteer for it, but I bought into it when I signed up for the Army.

QUESTIONS TO CONSIDER

1. Why are Captain Anderson and his men dispatched to the area near LZ Pink in the Central Highlands?

2. Why is Anderson an "absolute rarity" in Vietnam?

3. How do you think Anderson feels about his role in Vietnam?

The End
of the War

The Paris Accords

BY FLORA LEWIS

*In March 1967, Lyndon Johnson announced that he would not run
for another term as president. He was replaced by the conservative
Richard Nixon, who had run on the platform of "peace with honor."
Policies changed under Nixon. Peace talks in Paris, which had
begun in 1968, were expanded, and Nixon began to pull American
troops out of Vietnam. However, he accompanied this pullout with
increased bombing. The U.S. now wanted out of the war, but hoped
to make sure that South Vietnam could survive. As talks dragged
on, U.S. troops in Vietnam dropped from a high of 586,100 in
1968 down to 24,200 in 1972. An agreement was finally reached
in January of 1973 that provided for a **cessation**[1] of hostilities and
the pull-out of all American forces. The last U.S. troops left Vietnam
on March 29, 1973, bringing an end to America's longest war.
The following selection is a news report by Flora Lewis on the signing
of the Paris Accords.*

     PARIS, *Jan. 27*—The Vietnam cease-fire agreement
was signed here today in eerie silence, without a word

---

[1] **cessation**—a ceasing.

or a gesture to express the world's relief that the years of war were officially ending.

The accord was effective at 7 P.M. Eastern standard time.

Secretary of State William P. Rogers wrote his name 62 times on the documents providing—after 12 years—a settlement of the longest, most divisive foreign war in America's history.

The official title of the text was "Agreement on Ending the War and Restoring Peace in Vietnam." But the cold, almost gloomy atmosphere at two separate signing ceremonies reflected the uncertainties of whether peace is now **assured**.[2]

The conflict, which has raged in one way or another for over a quarter of a century, had been inconclusive, without clear victory or defeat for either side.

After a gradually increasing involvement that began even before France left Indochina in 1954, the United States entered into a full-scale combat role in 1965. The United States considers Jan. 1, 1961, as the war's starting date and casualties are counted from then.

By 1968, when the build-up was stopped and then reversed, there were 529,000 Americans fighting in Vietnam. United States dead passed 45,000 by the end of the war.

The peace agreements were as ambiguous as the conflict, which many of America's friends first saw as generous aid to a weak and threatened ally, but which many came to consider an exercise of brute power against a tiny nation.

The peace agreements signed today were built of compromises that permit the two Vietnamese sides to give them contradictory meanings and, they clearly hope, to continue their unfinished struggle in the political arena without continuing the slaughter.

---

[2] **assured**—certain.

The signing took place in two ceremonies. In the morning, the participants were the United States, North Vietnam, South Vietnam and the Vietcong. Because the Saigon Government does not wish to imply recognition of the Vietcong's Provisional Revolutionary Government, all references to that government were confined to a second set of documents. That set was signed in the afternoon, and by only the United States and North Vietnam.

At the last moment, it was found that two copies in English of the texts, which were to have been signed by Mr. Rogers and North Vietnam's Foreign Minister, Nguyen Duy Trinh, in the afternoon ceremony, were missing.

The plan had been to give a signed copy in each language to each of the four delegations. The United States prepared the English documents and had given the two copies to the South Vietnamese to inspect. They were not returned, leaving a total of six instead of eight sets of documents to be signed by the United States and North Vietnam.

These texts began by saying that North Vietnam "with the concurrence of the Provisional Revolutionary Government of the Republic of South Vietnam" and the United States "with the concurrence of the Government of the Republic of Vietnam" had reached agreement.

South Vietnam's foreign minister, Tran Van Lam, indicated that he did not want to accept signed copies of this text, because Saigon objects to mention of the revolutionary government by that name.

Asked whether the South Vietnamese action might weaken or undermine the degree of Saigon's "concurrence," American officials said, "No, no. They have concurred."

Each of the other delegations wound up with four sets of signed agreements. Saigon took only two, the English and Vietnamese versions mentioning only "parties" to the conference.

In the morning ceremony, all four parties signed identical agreements, except for one **protocol,**[3] or annexed document, in which the United States agreed to remove the mines it had planted in the waters of North Vietnam.

The preamble on the four-party documents mentioned no government by name and referred only to the "parties participating in the Paris conference on Vietnam."

That was the formula that had broken the final deadlock.

Almost immediately after the morning session involving four foreign ministers, military delegations of the Vietcong and the North Vietnamese flew off on their way to Saigon.

They, with American and South Vietnamese officers, will form a joint military commission that is to carry out the cease-fire. Their departure for the South Vietnamese capital gave a touch of reality to the strangely emotionless way in which the rite of peace was performed in Paris.

After the morning ceremony, which lasted 18 minutes, the four foreign ministers, their aides and guests filed wordlessly through separate doors into a curtained foyer.

There, participants said, they clinked champagne glasses, toasted "peace and friendship" and shook hands all around. But such amiability was concealed from observers and above all from the cameras that might have recorded a scene of the Vietnamese enemies in social contact.

A similar 15 minutes of cordiality followed the 11-minute afternoon ceremony, attended only by the American and North Vietnamese delegations.

The agreement was signed at the gigantic round table, covered with a prairie of green **baize,**[4] where the four parties to the Paris conference have been

---

[3] **protocol**—the first copy of a treaty or other such document before its ratification.

[4] **baize**—coarse felt-like fabric.

speechifying at each other, and often **vilifying**[5] each other, almost weekly for four years.

The great ballroom of the former Hotel Majestic, where the table stands, is crammed with crystal and gilt chandeliers, lush tapestries and ornate gilt moldings. But the scene was as glum as the drizzly, gray Paris sky outside. The men all wore dark suits.

The touches of human color were few. Mrs. Nguyen Thi Binh, Foreign Minister of the Vietcong Provisional Revolutionary Government, wore an amber ao dai[6] with embroidery on the bodice, an unusual ornament for her.

Mrs. Rogers wore a dress with a red top and navy skirt. In the afternoon when there were only two delegations and thus more room for guests, all the American secretaries who had been involved were brought in and they brightened the room.

The texts of the agreements were bound in different colored leather—red for the North Vietnamese, blue for the United States, brown for South Vietnam and green for the Vietcong. French ushers solemnly passed them around on each signature. Mrs. Binh overlooked one place to sign and had to be given an album back for completion.

Mr. Rogers and Mr. Trinh used a large number of the black pens and then handed them to delegation members as souvenirs. William J. Porter, the new Deputy Undersecretary of State who had been the United States delegate to the semi-public talks until this month, flew to Paris with Mr. Rogers and sat at the table with him.

Heywood Isham, acting head of the United States delegation, Marshall Green, Assistant Secretary of State for East Asian and Pacific Affairs, and William H. Sullivan, Mr. Green's deputy, who has been leading technical talks with the North Vietnamese here, completed the American group at the table.

---

[5] **vilifying**—making vicious and defamatory statements about.

[6] ao dai—traditional dress of Vietnamese women, consisting of a long tunic slit on the sides and worn over loose trousers.

Two rectangular tables, carefully placed alongside the main table to symbolize the separation of the four delegations into two warring sides at the start of the conference in 1969, were reserved for the ambassadors of Canada, Hungary, Indonesia and Poland.

Their countries are contributing troops to an international commission that is to supervise the cease-fire.

Mr. Rogers and his Washington-based aides flew home immediately after the ceremony. Unexpectedly, Mr. Lam went with them.

Mr. Sullivan remained in Paris to receive the list of American prisoners from Hanoi and to hold further technical meetings on the many unsettled details of how arrangements are to be carried out.

At the airport before leaving, Mr. Rogers made his only comments on the event so long awaited with spurts of hope and bitter despair.

"It's a great day," he said.

He said President Nixon had devoted himself to building a structure of peace and continued: "The events in Paris today are a milestone in achieving that peace."

"I hope there'll be a cease-fire soon in all of Indochina," he added.

QUESTIONS TO CONSIDER

1. What was uncertain about the peace agreements?

2. What did the drafters of the peace agreement need to do to break the deadlock in negotiations between North Vietnam, South Vietnam, the Viet Cong, and the U.S.?

3. Why do you think the mood of the peace accords was so gloomy?

The Fall of Saigon

BY VAN TIEN DUNG

The Paris Accords did not bring an end to the war in Vietnam. Despite the accords' call for a cease-fire, North and South Vietnam went right back to war. In the spring of 1975, South Vietnamese forces finally collapsed, and Saigon was captured by the North. After more than thirty years of war, Vietnam was whole and independent. General Van Tien Dung commanded the North Vietnamese invasion of the South in 1974–75. His book Our Great Spring Victory *describes the conquest of South Vietnam. This selection from Dung's book describes the taking of Saigon.*

When it was almost light, the American news services reported that [U.S. Ambassador Graham] Martin had cleared out of Saigon in a helicopter. This viceregal[1] mandarin, the final American plenipotentiary[2] in South Vietnam, beat a most hasty and pitiful retreat. As it

---

[1] viceregal—of or relating to a viceroy, a man who is the governor of a country, province, or colony, ruling as the representative of a sovereign.

[2] plenipotentiary—diplomatic agent, such as an ambassador, fully authorized to represent his or her government.

happened, up until the day he left Saigon, Martin still felt certain that the quisling[3] administration could be preserved, and that a ceasefire could be arranged, so he was halfhearted about the evacuation, waiting and watching. He went all the way out to Tan Son Nhat airfield to observe the situation. Our barrage of bombs and our fierce shelling had nearly paralyzed this vital airfield, and the fixed-wing aircraft they had intended to use for their evacuation could no longer operate. The encirclement of Saigon was growing tighter by the day. The Duong Van Minh card which they had played far too late proved useless. When Martin reported this to Washington, President Ford issued orders to begin a helicopter evacuation. Coming in waves for eighteen hours straight, they carried more than 1,000 Americans and over 5,000 of their Vietnamese retainers, along with their families, out of the South. Ford also ordered Martin to evacuate immediately "without a minute's delay."

The American evacuation was carried out from the tops of thirteen tall buildings chosen as landing pads for their helicopters. The number of these landing pads shrank gradually as tongues of fire from our advancing troops came closer. At the American embassy, the boarding point for the evacuation copters was a scene of monumental confusion, with the Americans' flunkies[4] fighting their way in, smashing doors, climbing walls, climbing each other's backs, tussling, brawling, and trampling each other as they sought to flee. It reached the point where Martin, who wanted to return to his own house for his suitcase before he fled, had to take a back street, using the rear gate of the embassy. When "Code 2," Martin's code name, and "Lady 09,"

---

[3] quisling—like a traitor who serves as the puppet of the enemy occupying his or her country.

[4] flunkies—people of slavish or unquestioning obedience; lackeys.

the name of the helicopter carrying him, left the embassy for the East Sea, it signaled the shameful defeat of U.S. imperialism after thirty years of intervention and military adventures in Vietnam. At the height of their invasion of Vietnam, the U.S. had used 60 percent of their total infantry, 58 percent of their marines, 32 percent of their tactical air force, 50 percent of their strategic air force, fifteen of their eighteen aircraft carriers, 800,000 American troops (counting those stationed in satellite countries who were taking part in the Vietnam war), and more than 1 million Saigon troops. They mobilized as many as 6 million American soldiers in rotation, dropped over 10 million tons of bombs, and spent over $300 billion, but in the end the U.S. ambassador had to crawl up to the helicopter pad looking for a way to flee. Today, looking back on the gigantic force the enemy had mobilized, recalling the malicious designs they admitted, and thinking about the extreme difficulties and complexities which our revolutionary sampan[5] had had to pass through, we were all the more aware how immeasurably great this campaign to liberate Saigon and liberate the South was. . . .

The most extraordinary thing about this historic campaign was what had sprouted in the souls of our cadres and fighters. Why were our soldiers so heroic and determined during this campaign? What had given all of them this clear understanding of the great resolution of the party and of the nation, this clear understanding of our immeasurably precious opportunity, and this clear understanding of our unprecedented manner of fighting? What had made them so extraordinarily courageous and intense, so

---

[5] sampan—a flat-bottomed Asian skiff usually propelled by two oars, used figuratively here.

outstanding in their political **acumen**[6] in this final phase of the war?

The will and competence of our soldiers were not achieved in a day, but were the result of a continuous process of carrying out the party's ideological and organizational work in the armed forces. And throughout our thirty years of struggle, there had been no campaign in which Uncle Ho had not gone into the operation with our soldiers. Going out to battle this time, our whole army had been given singular, unprecedented strength because this strategically decisive battle bore his name: Ho Chi Minh, for every one of our cadres and fighters, was faith, strength, and life. Among the myriad troops in all the advancing wings, every one of our fighters carried toward Ho Chi Minh City the hopes of the nation and a love for our land. Today each fighter could see with his own eyes the resiliency which the Fatherland had built up during these many years, and given his own resiliency there was nothing, no enemy scheme that could stop him.

Our troops advanced rapidly to the five primary objectives, and then spread out from there. Wherever they went, a forest of revolutionary flags appeared, and people poured out to cheer them, turning the streets of Saigon into a giant festival. From the Binh Phoc bridge to Quan Tre, people carrying flags, beating drums and hollow wooden fish, and calling through megaphones, chased down the enemy, disarmed enemy soldiers, neutralized traitors and spies, and guided our soldiers. In Hoc Mon on Route 1, the people all came out into the road to greet the soldiers, guide them, and point out the hiding places of enemy thugs. Everywhere people used megaphones to call on Saigon soldiers to take off their uniforms and lay down their guns. The people of the

---

[6] **acumen**—keenness of perception.

city, especially the workers, protected factories and warehouses and turned them over to our soldiers. In all the districts bordering the city—Binh Hoa, Thanh My Tay, Phu Nhuan, Go Vap, and Thu Duc—members of the revolutionary **infrastructure**[7] and other people distributed leaflets, raised flags, called on enemy soldiers to drop their guns, and supplied and guided our soldiers. Before this great army entered the city, the great cause of our nation and the policies of our revolution had entered the hearts of the people.

We were very pleased to hear that the people of the city rose up when the military attacks, going one step ahead, had given them the leverage. The masses had entered this decisive battle at just the right time, not too early, but not too late. The patriotic actions of the people created a revolutionary atmosphere of vast strength on all the city's streets. This was the most precious aspect of the mass movement in Saigon-Gia Dinh, the result of many years of propaganda, education, organizing, and training by the municipal party branch. When the **opportune**[8] moment arrived, those political troops had risen up with a vanguard spirit, and advanced in giant strides along with our powerful main-force divisions, resolutely, intelligently, and courageously. The people of the city not only carried flags and food and drink for the troops, but helped disperse large numbers of enemy soldiers, forced many to surrender, chased and captured many of those who were hiding out, and preserved order and security in the streets. And we will never forget the widespread and moving images of thousands, of tens of thousands of people enthusiastically giving directions to our soldiers and guiding them as they entered the city, and helping all the wings of troops

---

[7] **infrastructure**—an underlying base or foundation especially for an organization or a system.

[8] **opportune**—suited or right for a particular purpose.

strike quickly and unexpectedly at enemy positions. Those nameless heroes of Saigon-Gia Dinh brought into the general offensive the fresh and beautiful features of people's war.

As we looked at the combat operations map, the five wings of our troops seemed like five lotuses blossoming out from our five major objectives. The First Army Corps had captured Saigon's General Staff headquarters and the command compounds of all the enemy armed services. When the Third Army Corps captured Tan Son Nhat they met one wing of troops already encamped there—our military delegation at Camp Davis; it was an amazing and moving meeting. The Fourth Army Corps captured Saigon's Ministry of Defense, the Bach Dang port, and the radio station. The 232nd force took the Special Capital Zone headquarters and the Directorate-General of Police. The Second Army Corps seized "Independence Palace," the place where the quisling leaders, those hirelings of the United States, had sold our independence, traded in human blood, and carried on their smuggling. Our soldiers immediately rushed upstairs to the place where the quisling cabinet was meeting, and arrested the whole central leadership of the Saigon administration, including their president, right on the spot. Our soldiers' vigorous actions and firm declarations revealed the spirit of a victorious army. By 11:30 A.M. on April 30 the revolutionary flag flew from "Independence Palace"; this became the meeting point for all the wings of liberating troops.

At the front headquarters, we turned on our radios to listen. The voice of the quisling president called on his troops to put down their weapons and surrender unconditionally to our troops. Saigon was completely liberated! Total victory! We were completely victorious!

All of us at headquarters jumped up and shouted, embraced and carried each other around on our shoulders. The sound of applause, laughter, and happy, noisy, chattering speech was as festive as if spring had just burst upon us. It was an indescribably joyous scene. Le Duc Tho and Pham Hung embraced me and all the cadres and fighters present. We were all so happy we were choked with emotion. I lit a cigarette and smoked. Dinh Duc Thien, his eyes somewhat red, said, "Now if these eyes close, my heart will be at rest." This historic and sacred, intoxicating and completely satisfying moment was one that comes once in a generation, once in many generations. Our generation had known many victorious mornings, but there had been no morning so fresh and beautiful, so radiant, so clear and cool, so sweet-scented as this morning of total victory, a morning which made babes older than their years and made old men young again. . . .

Le Duc Tho, Pham Hung, and I leaned on our chairs looking at the map of Ho Chi Minh City spread out on the table. We thought of the welter of jobs ahead. Were the electricity and water still working? Saigon's army of nearly 1 million had disbanded on the spot. How should we deal with them? What could we do to help the hungry and find ways for the millions of unemployed to make a living? Should we ask the center to send in supplies right away to keep the factories in Saigon alive? How could we quickly build up a revolutionary administration at the grass-roots level? What policy should we take toward the **bourgeoisie?**[9] And how could we carry the South on to socialism along with the whole country? The conclusion of this struggle was the opening of another, no less complex and filled with hardship. The difficulties would be many, but the

---

[9] **bourgeoisie**—middle class.

advantages were not few. Saigon and the South, which had gone out first and returned last, deserved a life of peace, plenty, and happiness. . . .

On May 1 . . . [we] took a car to Saigon, past areas and positions so vital for the liberation of the city, like Trang Bang and Cu Chi, and past areas which had been revolutionary bases for many years, since the founding of the party, like Hoc Mon and Ba Diem. Along the highway, in the villages, and in the city streets there was no sea of blood, only a sea of people in high spirits, waving their hands and waving flags to welcome peace and the revolution. That sea of people, mingling endlessly with the long lines of our soldiers' trucks, tanks, and cars, in itself proclaimed our total victory. The sides of the road were still clogged with uniforms, rank insignia, guns and ammunition, boots, helmets, vehicles, and artillery the puppet army had abandoned in defeat. Spread out around us were not only the relics of a military force that had been smashed, but the relics of a reactionary political doctrine that had unraveled, the doctrine of a crew of imperialists so arrogant about their wealth and so worshipful of possessions that it blinded them. It was ironic that at every enemy base and barracks a sign had been erected, painted in large letters with the words, "Honor—Responsibility—Fatherland." What the enemy did not have, they had to shout about loudest. The main road to Saigon was very good, built by the enemy in the past to serve their operations. All of the enemy bases and storage depots were vast. The banks, the American **billets,**[10] the hotels, many stories tall, were imposing advertisements for neocolonialism, implying that it would stand firm here, that it would stand for time without end. In 1968 Westmoreland boasted, "We will always be in Vietnam. Our bombs and bullets will prove it."

---

[10] **billets**—lodgings for soldiers.

But in fact the proof was exactly the opposite. We went into the headquarters of Saigon's General Staff. Here, as at the enemy Directorate-General of Police, the files of the enemy commanders' top secret documents remained. Their modern computer with its famous memory containing bio-data on each officer and soldier in their million-plus army was still running. American computers had not won in this war. The intelligence and will of our nation had won completely.

QUESTIONS TO CONSIDER

1. Why does the fall of Saigon mark the end of the war between North and South Vietnam?

2. How does Van Tien Dung feel about the "enemy"—the people of South Vietnam?

3. Why does Van Tien Dung keep repeating how thrilled the people of Saigon were to see the North Vietnamese troops?

Epilogue

from

In Country

BY BOBBIE ANN MASON

A visit to the Vietnam Veterans Memorial in Washington, D.C., is the climax of the novel In Country *(1985) by Bobbie Ann Mason. In the novel Sam Hughes, a teenage girl whose father was killed in Vietnam, her grandmother and her Uncle Emmett, another veteran, travel to see Sam's father's name on the memorial. It is an important moment for all three in coming to terms with what Vietnam has meant to them: for Sam, the loss of a father; for Mamaw, the loss of a son; and for Emmett, an inexplicable whirl of emotions and events. The following selection is from the final chapter of* In Country.

. . . Sam feels sick with apprehension. She has kept telling herself that the memorial is only a rock with names on it. It doesn't mean anything except they're dead. It's just names. Nobody here but us chickens. Just us and the planet Earth and the nuclear bomb. But that's O.K., she thinks now. There is something comforting about the idea of nobody here but us chickens. It's so intimate. Nobody here but us. Maybe that's the point. People shouldn't make too much of death. Her history teacher said there are more people alive now than dead. He warned that there were so many people alive now, and they were living so much longer, that people had the idea they were practically immortal. But everyone's going to die and we'd better get used to the notion, he said. Dead and gone. Long gone from Kentucky.

Sometimes in the middle of the night it struck Sam with sudden clarity that she was going to die someday. Most of the time she forgot about this. But now, as she and Emmett and Mamaw Hughes drive into Washington, where the Vietnam Memorial bears the names of so many who died, the reality of death hits her in broad daylight. Mamaw is fifty-eight. She is going to die soon. She could die any minute, like that racehorse that keeled over dead, inexplicably, on Father's Day. Sam has been so afraid Emmett would die. But Emmett came to Cawood's Pond looking for her, because it was unbearable to him that she might have left him alone, that she might even die.

The Washington Monument is a gleaming pencil against the sky. Emmett is driving, and the traffic is frightening, so many cars swishing and merging, like bold skaters in a crowded rink. They pass cars with government license plates that say F E D. Sam wonders how long the Washington Monument will stand on the Earth.

A brown sign on Constitution Avenue says V I E T-N A M   V E T E R A N S   M E M O R I A L. Emmett can't find a parking place nearby. He parks on a side street and they walk toward the Washington Monument. Mamaw puffs along. She has put on a good dress and stockings. Sam feels they are ambling, out for a stroll, it is so slow. She wants to break into a run. The Washington Monument rises up out of the earth, proud and tall. . . .

In Washington, the buildings are so pretty, so white. In a dream, the Vietnam Memorial was a black boomerang, whizzing toward her head.

"I don't see it," Mamaw says.

"It's over yonder," Emmett says, pointing. "They say you come up on it sudden."

"My legs are starting to hurt."

Sam wants to run, but she doesn't know whether she wants to run toward the memorial or away from it. She just wants to run. She has the new record album with her, so it won't melt in the hot car. It's in a plastic bag with handles. Emmett is carrying the pot of geraniums. She is amazed by him, his impressive bulk, his secret suffering. She feels his anxiety. His heart must be racing, as if something intolerable is about to happen.

Emmett holds Mamaw's arm protectively and steers her across the street. The pot of geraniums hugs his chest.

"There it is," Sam says.

It is massive, a black gash in a hillside, like a vein of coal exposed and then polished with polyurethane. A crowd is filing by slowly, staring at it solemnly.

"Law," says Sam's grandmother quietly. "It's black as night."

"Here's the directory," Emmett says, pausing at the entrance. "I'll look up his name for you, Mrs. Hughes."

The directory is on a pedestal with a protective plastic shield. Sam stands in the shade, looking forward, at the black wing embedded in the soil, with grass growing above. It is like a giant grave, fifty-eight thousand bodies rotting here behind those names. The people are streaming past, down into the pit.

"It don't show up good," Mamaw says anxiously. "It's just a hole in the ground."

The memorial cuts a V in the ground, like the wings of an abstract bird, huge and headless. Overhead, a jet plane angles upward, taking off.

"It's on Panel 9 E ," Emmett reports. "That's on the east wing. We're on the west."

At the bottom of the wall is a granite trough, and on the edge of it the sunlight reflects the names just above, in mirror writing, upside down. Flower arrangements are scattered at the base. A little kid says, "Look, Daddy, the flowers are dying." The man snaps, "Some are and some aren't."

The walkway is separated from the memorial by a strip of gravel, and on the other side of the walk is a border of dark gray brick. The shiny surface of the wall reflects the Lincoln Memorial and the Washington Monument, at opposite angles.

A woman in a sunhat is focusing a camera on the wall. She says to the woman with her, "I didn't think it would look like this. Things aren't what you think they look like. I didn't know it was a wall. "

A spraddle-legged guy in camouflage clothing walks by with a cane. Probably he has an artificial leg, Sam thinks, but he walks along proudly, as if he has been here many times before and doesn't have any particular business at that moment. He seems to belong here, like Emmett hanging out at McDonald's.

A group of schoolkids tumble through, noisy as chickens. As they enter, one of the girls says, "Are they piled on top of each other?" They walk a few steps farther and she says, "What are all these names anyway?" Sam feels like punching the girl in the face for being so dumb. How could anybody that age not know? But she realizes that she doesn't know either. She is just beginning to understand. And she will never really know what happened to all these men in the war. Some people walk by, talking as though they are on a Sunday picnic, but most are reverent, and some of them are crying.

Sam stands in the center of the V, deep in the pit. The V is like the white wings of the shopping mall in Paducah.[1] The Washington Monument is reflected at the center line. If she moves slightly to the left, she sees the monument, and if she moves the other way she sees a reflection of the flag opposite the memorial. Both the monument and the flag seem like arrogant gestures, like the country giving the finger to the dead boys, flung in this hole in the ground. Sam doesn't understand what she is feeling, but it is something so strong, it is like a tornado moving in her, something massive and over-powering. It feels like giving birth to this wall.

"I wish Tom could be here," Sam says to Emmett. "He needs to be here." Her voice is thin, like smoke, barely audible.

"He'll make it here someday. Jim's coming too. They're all coming one of these days."

"Are you going to look for anybody's name besides my daddy's?"

"Yeah."

"Who?"

"Those guys I told you about, the ones that died all around me that day. And that guy I was going to look up—he might be here. I don't know if he made it out or not."

Sam gets a flash of Emmett's suffering, his grieving all these years. He has been grieving for fourteen years. In this dazzling sunlight, his pimples don't show. A jet plane flies overhead, close to the earth. Its wings are angled back too, like a bird's.

Two workmen in hard hats are there with a steplad-der and some loud machinery. One of the workmen, whose hat says on the back NEVER AGAIN, seems to be drilling into the wall.

"What's he doing, hon?" Sam hears Mamaw say behind her.

---

[1] Paducah—a city in western Kentucky on the Ohio River.

"It looks like they're patching up a hole or something." *Fixing a hole where the rain gets in.*

The man on the ladder turns off the tool, a sander, and the other workman hands him a brush. He brushes the spot. Silver duct tape is patched around several names, leaving the names exposed. The names are highlighted in yellow, as though someone has taken a Magic Marker and colored them, the way Sam used to mark names and dates, important facts, in her textbooks.

"Somebody must have vandalized it," says a man behind Sam. "Can you imagine the sicko who would do that?"

"No," says the woman with him. "Somebody just wanted the names to stand out and be noticed. I can go with that."

"Do you think they colored Dwayne's name?" Mamaw asks Sam worriedly.

"No. Why would they?" Sam gazes at the flowers spaced along the base of the memorial. A white carnation is stuck in a crack between two panels of the wall. A woman bends down and straightens a ribbon on a wreath. The ribbon has gold letters on it, "VFW Post 7215 of Pa."

They are moving slowly. Panel 9 E is some distance ahead. Sam reads a small poster propped at the base of the wall: "To those men of C Company, 1st Bn. 503 Inf., 173rd Airborne who were lost in the battle for Hill 823, Dak To, Nov. 11, 1967. Because of their bravery I am here today. A grateful buddy."

A man rolls past in a wheelchair. Another jet plane flies over.

A handwritten note taped to the wall apologizes to one of the names for abandoning him in a firefight.

Mamaw turns to fuss over the geraniums in Emmett's arms, the way she might fluff a pillow.

The workmen are cleaning the yellow paint from the names. They sand the wall and brush it carefully, like men polishing their cars. The man on the ladder sprays water on the name he has just sanded and wipes it with a rag.

Sam, conscious of how slowly they are moving, with dread, watches two uniformed marines searching and searching for a name. "He must have been along here somewhere," one says. They keep looking, running their hands over the names.

"There it is. That's him."

They read his name and both look abruptly away, stare out for a moment in the direction of the Lincoln Memorial, then walk briskly off.

"May I help you find someone's name?" asks a woman in a T-shirt and green pants. She is a park guide, with a clipboard in her hand.

"We know where we are," Emmett says. "Much obliged, though. "

At panel 9E, Sam stands back while Emmett and Mamaw search for her father's name. Emmett, his gaze steady and intent, faces the wall, as though he were watching birds; and Mamaw, through her glasses, seems intent and purposeful, as though she were looking for something back in the field, watching to see if a cow had gotten out of the pasture. Sam imagines the egret[2] patrolling for ticks on a water buffalo's back, ducking and snaking its head forward, its beak like a punji stick.

"There it is," Emmett says. It is far above his head, near the top of the wall. He reaches up and touches the name. "There's his name, Dwayne E. Hughes."

"I can't reach it," says Mamaw. "Oh, I wanted to touch it," she says softly, in disappointment.

---

[2] egret—long-necked wading bird.

"We'll set the flowers here, Mrs. Hughes," says Emmett. He sets the pot at the base of the panel, tenderly, as though tucking in a baby.

"I'm going to bawl," Mamaw says, bowing her head and starting to sob. "I wish I could touch it."

Sam has an idea. She sprints over to the workmen and asks them to let her borrow the stepladder. They are almost finished, and they agree. One of them brings it over and sets it up beside the wall, and Sam urges Mamaw to climb the ladder, but Mamaw protests. "No, I can't do it. You do it."

"Go ahead, ma'am," the workman says.

"Emmett and me'll hold the ladder," says Sam.

"Somebody might see up my dress."

"No, go on, Mrs. Hughes. You can do it," says Emmett. "Come on, we'll help you reach it."

He takes her arm. Together, he and Sam steady her while she places her foot on the first step and swings herself up. She seems scared, and she doesn't speak. She reaches but cannot touch the name.

"One more, Mamaw," says Sam, looking up at her grandmother—at the sagging wrinkles, her flab hanging loose and sad, and her eyes reddened with crying. Mamaw reaches toward the name and slowly struggles up the next step, holding her dress tight against her. She touches the name, running her hand over it, stroking it tentatively, affectionately, like feeling a cat's back. Her chin wobbles, and after a moment she backs down the ladder silently.

When Mamaw is down, Sam starts up the ladder, with the record package in her hand.

"Here, take the camera, Sam. Get his name." Mamaw has brought Donna's Instamatic.

"No, I can't take a picture this close."

Sam climbs the ladder until she is eye level with her father's name. She feels funny, touching it. A scratching on a rock. Writing. Something for future archaeologists to puzzle over, clues to a language.

"Look this way, Sam," Mamaw says. "I want to take your picture. I want to get you and his name and the flowers in together if I can."

"The name won't show up," Sam says.

"Smile."

"How can I smile?" She is crying.

Mamaw backs up and snaps two pictures. Sam feels her face looking blank. Up on the ladder, she feels so tall, like a spindly weed that is sprouting up out of this diamond-bright seam of hard earth. She sees Emmett at the directory, probably searching for his buddies' names. She touches her father's name again.

"All I can see here is my reflection,"' Mamaw says when Sam comes down the ladder, "I hope his name shows up. And your face was all shadow."

"Wait here a minute," Sam says, turning away her tears from Mamaw. She hurries to the directory on the east side. Emmett isn't there anymore. She sees him striding along the wall, looking for a certain panel, Nearby, a group of marines is keeping a vigil for the POWs and MIAs. A double row of flags is planted in the dirt alongside their table. One of the marines walks by with a poster, "You Are an American, Your Voice Can Make the Difference." Sam flips through the directory and finds "Hughes." She wants to see her father's name there too. She runs down the row of Hughes names. There were so many Hughes boys killed, names she doesn't know. His name is there, and she gazes at it for a moment. Then suddenly her own name leaps out at her.

SAM ALAN HUGHES PFC AR 02 MAR 49 02 FEB 67 HOUSTON TX 14E 104

Her heart pounding, she rushes to panel 14E, and after racing her eyes over the string of names for a moment, she locates her own name.

SAM A HUGHES. It is the first on a line. It is down low enough to touch. She touches her own name. How odd it feels, as though all the names in America have been used to decorate this wall.

Mamaw is there at her side, clutching at Sam's arm, digging in with her fingernails. Mamaw says, "Coming up on this wall of a sudden and seeing how black it was, it was so awful, but then I came down in it and saw that white carnation blooming out of that crack and it gave me hope. It made me know he's watching over us." She loosens her bird-claw grip. "Did we lose Emmett?"

Silently, Sam points to the place where Emmett is studying the names low on a panel. He is sitting there cross-legged in front of the wall, and slowly his face bursts into a smile like flames.

QUESTIONS TO CONSIDER

1. Why is Sam so nervous about seeing the Veterans Memorial for the first time?

2. Why do you think Mamaw wants to touch her son's name?

3. How does Sam feel after she finds her father's name?

4. How does she feel when she finds her own name?

Can Vietnam Forget?

BY KEVIN WHITELAW

Nearly quarter of a century after the end of the war, journalist Kevin Whitelaw returned to Vietnam to report on how the Vietnamese people remember the war and how they feel now about America. In visiting the War Remnants Museum and looking at the way the war was taught in schools, Whitelaw finds the accepted Communist view of the war, but also a highly complex view of Americans' guilt and a willingness to consider reconciliation.

HANOI—Like many teenagers, Minh, 18, likes to play video games. In one of his favorites, he pilots an American fighter plane and shoots down Vietnamese jets. In another, he kills Vietnamese and Soviet troops with a knife and then bombs the jungle to save American advisers. Minh's father, who entered Saigon with the North Vietnamese Army in 1975, simply shrugs. "It's just a game," he says.

Twenty-three years after the fall of Saigon and the evacuation of the U.S. Embassy, the Vietnamese view of the war is changing. An estimated 65 percent of the population was born after hostilities ended. Many of these young Vietnamese are, if not as blithely indifferent as Minh, certainly less ideological than the Communist Party would like. The party continues to purvey its view of the war in school textbooks, and it recently launched a propaganda offensive to make sure that the costly victory is not forgotten. But a host of evidence—from new books to museum exhibits and university lectures—indicates that Vietnam is losing its bitterness toward America, seeing the war somewhat more objectively, and gaining a fuller understanding of why U.S. troops were sent to fight. From the late 1970s through the '80s, the American War Crimes Museum in Ho Chi Minh City (formerly Saigon) was the centerpiece of war propaganda. Photographs showed American GIs with dead Vietnamese soldiers and civilians, and the accompanying text said the Americans "seem satisfied" with their work.

New name. Today, Nguyen Tuyet Van, director of the renamed War Remnants Museum, giggles when asked about the old captions. "We try to make the exhibition very objective," she says, noting that the museum has been extensively renovated in the past five years. "We use the explanations provided by the Western photographers." Indeed, most of the exhibit about the U.S. massacre of civilians at My Lai was taken from a 1969 article in *Life* magazine.

The museum—visited by 2,000 schoolchildren a day—remains a provocative depiction of American conduct during the war. Along with pictures of dead civilians, decapitated soldiers, and napalmed villages, it features a jar filled with the embalmed remains of a deformed baby, allegedly poisoned by the defoliant Agent Orange. But the captions, for the most part, are straightforward, and a new section is dedicated to the U.S. antiwar movement.

Historians also teach a more **nuanced**[1] view of American motives. "In 1977, we only lectured on what we were given and, of course, there were materials about American colonialism," says Nguyen Dinh Le, a war historian at Vietnam National University in Hanoi. "Now, I tell my students that the main reason the U.S. government wanted to invade Vietnam was under its global strategy against communism."

This revision reflects some self-interest. Vietnam needs American investment, especially with the rest of Asia mired in economic crisis. "During wartime, our historians wrote the history to serve the struggle," says Le Van Quang, dean of history at Vietnam National University in Ho Chi Minh City.

"We still write about the war, but we try to find things to serve our two countries."

Desire for foreign investment, however, cannot explain the change in popular novels. For years, they portrayed the war exclusively in heroic terms. Even love was patriotic; women were always faithful to men at the front, and **valorous**[2] soldiers returned to honor and gratitude. Only in the 1980s did suffering and betrayal begin to appear in these epics. One of Vietnam's best-known novels, Bao Ninh's 1991 *The Sorrow of War*, tells the story of a soldier who returns from the war to find his work, family, and love life in ruins. But this remains a touchy topic. Although originally published in Vietnam, the book has since been banned. It is now available only from street peddlers in a bootleg English-language edition. Interest in America. American movies are popular in Vietnam, especially among the young. Even the Vietnam War movie *Platoon* played in Hanoi. But it was not until 1995 that the first **nonpolemical**[3] book about life in America was pub-

---

[1] **nuanced**—subtle.

[2] **valorous**—brave; decorated.

[3] **nonpolemical**—uncontroversial.

lished. *A File on American Culture* by Huu Ngoc ranges across the U.S. landscape from the Ku Klux Klan to the beatnik generation, gays and lesbians, and the puzzling American obsession with eliminating body odors. Before this volume became a bestseller, says Huu, "Americans were always presented as devils." Today, resentment of Americans is difficult to find. A "hero mother," who lost three of her four sons during the war, warmly received an American reporter in her home and brought out family photos. Pete Peterson, the U.S. ambassador to Vietnam and a former prisoner of war at the infamous "Hanoi Hilton," says he has not experienced any lingering hatred. A few months ago, Peterson met Nguyen Viet Chop, the North Vietnamese soldier who captured him during the war. "The only thing he asked me to help him do was to get his kids into school in the States," says Peterson. "They see an education in the States as the ticket to success." This unofficial forgiving and partial forgetting, however, is in tension with the Communist Party's glorification of victory. And the tension is **exacerbated**[4] by economic hardship. In the big cities, hotels are nearly empty, despite discounts of up to 50 percent. Unemployment is at least 11 percent, the average wage is just $1 per day, and scores of representatives of foreign companies have given up on Vietnam's bureaucracy and returned home. The party's reaction has been to remind the nation of its leadership in the war. "Without the war, they have nothing to reinforce their power," says a Vietnamese professor who asked not to be named. "They have only one accomplishment to claim— the victory." State radio and T V continually broadcast documentaries about the war days. "Hero mothers" appear in public ceremonies with growing frequency. And universities were told in June to boost the hours that students must spend on Marxism and Leninism.

---

[4] **exacerbated**—aggravated.

The history of the war is taught in the fifth, ninth, and twelfth grades, and all the textbooks still describe "American imperialists" who tried to occupy and enslave Vietnam. Similar rhetoric remains in Hanoi's Army Museum, where a sign claims that American and South Vietnamese forces raped 20,000 women and "operated on and took out the livers and eyes, then buried alive over 500,000 people."

While American atrocities—real or imagined—are widely reported, no one dares to challenge the purity of North Vietnamese motives and actions in the war. "For us, this was a just war to defend our country, so our Army couldn't have committed any crimes," says Nguyen, the director of the War Remnants Museum. The party is reluctant to admit even tactical errors on the battlefield. "You can't lose 3 million people in a conflict and have done everything right," says Peterson, the American ambassador. "But the history is too young, and too many of the participants are still here." Perhaps the most sensitive question is whether the conflict was, in any sense, a true civil war. American historians generally view it as a conflict between North and South, with Soviet backing for the North and American backing for the South. But the official Vietnamese version is that the South was nothing but a "puppet" of the United States. Any discussion of popular South Vietnamese aspirations for democracy is **anathema**.[5]

While the government often blames Vietnam's problems on the war, teachers **absolve**[6] ordinary Americans by distinguishing between the U.S. government and the American people, which is fully in keeping with Marxist-Leninist dogma. "In the lessons about this war, our teachers mention a lot about the antiwar movement,"

---

[5] **anathema**—something that is odious or disliked intensely.

[6] **absolve**—to pronounce clear of guilt or blame.

says Tran Nhu Thanh Tam, an education official in Ho Chi Minh City. "We consider that this represents the viewpoint of many American people during the war."

A **seminal**[7] event for Vietnamese historians was the publication in 1996 of former Secretary of Defense Robert McNamara's memoir, *In Retrospect*. Vietnamese historians regularly cite the book, and the War Remnants Museum quotes from McNamara's prologue in its brochure: "Yet we were wrong, terribly wrong. We owe it to future generations to explain why." McNamara's mea culpa[8] may gratify some Vietnamese Communists and reinforce their worldview. But it also excites admiration for America's openness and, according to one former Vietnamese diplomat, has made reconciliation easier.

---

[7] **seminal**—highly influential in an original way.

[8] mea culpa—plea or confession of guilt.

QUESTIONS TO CONSIDER

1. How have Vietnamese attitudes toward the U.S. changed since the end of the war?

2. Does the Communist Party approve of the "unofficial forgiving and partial forgetting" that is a part of Vietnamese culture today?

3. Was the Vietnam War a true civil war between North and South Vietnam, or was it more than that? Use what you've read to help you decide.

10 "Ambush" from *The Things They Carried*. Copyright © 1990 by Tim O'Brien. Reprinted by permission of Houghton Mifflin Co./Seymour Lawrence. All rights reserved.

16 Excerpts from "Settlement at Geneva—Then and Now," by Bernard B. Fall, *The New York Times*, May 2, 1965. Copyright © 1965 by The New York Times Co. Reprinted by permission.

24 From "Diem Defeats His Own Best Troops" by Stanley Karnow as appeared in *The Reporter*, January 19, 1961. Reprinted by permission of the author.

32 Excerpts from "A 'Very Real War' in Vietnam — and the Deep U.S. Commitment" by Homer Bigart, *The New York Times*, February 25, 1962. Copyright © 1962 by The New York Times Co. Reprinted by permission.

56 From *If I Die In A Combat Zone* by TIm O'Brien. Copyright © 1973 by Tim O'Brien. Used by permission of Delacorte Press/Seymour Lawrence, a division of Random House Inc.

68 From "Death in the Ia Drang Valley" by Specialist 4/C Jack P. Smith as appeared in *The Saturday Evening Post*, January 28, 1967.

74 From *Dispatches* by Michael Herr. Copyright © 1968, 1969, 1970, 1977 by Michael Herr. Reprinted by permission of Alfred A. Knopf Inc.

86 Excerpt from "The U.S. Negro in Vietnam" by Thomas A. Johnson, *The New York Times*, April 29, 1968. Copyright © 1968 by The New York Times Co. Reprinted by permission.

101 Excerpt by Maureen Walsh. Reprinted with permission from *A Piece Of My Heart* edited by Keith Walker. Reprinted by permission of Presidio Press, Navato, CA.

108 Excerpts from *Dear America: Letters Home from Vietnam* edited by Bernard Edelman for the New York Vietnam Veterans Memorial Commission, published by W.W. Norton & Company, 1985. Reprinted by permission of Bernard Edelman.

120 "The Next Step" reprinted from *Beautiful Wreckage: New & Selected Poems* by W. D. Ehrhart, Adastra Press, 1999, by permission of the author.

120 "Mines" from *A Romance*, by Bruce Weigl, © 1979. Reprinted by permission of the University of Pittsburgh Press.

121, 122 "Somewhere Near Phu Bai" and "Roll Call" from *Dien Cai Dau* by Yusef Komunyakaa. © 1988 by Yusef Komunyakaa, Wesleyan University Press by permission of University Press of New England.

130 Excerpted from "A Viet Cong" by Susan Sheehan. Appears in *Ten Vietnamese*. Copyright © 1966, 1967 by Susan Sheehan. This usage granted by permission of Lescher & Lescher, Ltd.

143 "Eight Dedicated Men Marked for Death" by Don Moser, *Life* Magazine, September 3, 1965. © 1965 Time Inc. Reprinted by permission.

153 Selection from "Life in the Maquis" in *A Vietcong Memoir* by Truong Nhu Tang, copyright © 1985 by Truong Nhu Tang, David Chanoff, and Doan Van Toai, reprinted by permission of Harcourt Brace & Company.

159 Excerpt from *One Very Hot Day* by David Halberstam. Copyright © 1967, renewed 1995 by David Halbertsam. Reprinted by permission of Houghton Mifflin Co. All rights reserved.

167 From *When Heaven And Earth Changed Places* by Le Ly Hayslip. Copyright © 1989 by Le Ly Hayslip and Charles Jay Wurts. Used by permission of Doubleday, a division of Random House Inc.

184 From Michael Ferber and Staughton Lynd, *The Resistance* (Boston: Beacon Press, 1971), p. 90.

188 "Afterthoughts on a Napalm-Drop in Jungle Villages Near Haiphong" by Barbara Beidler. Reprinted by permission of Barbara Beidler Kendrick.

189 "Truth Blazes Even in Little Children's Hearts" by Huy Can (translated from the Vietnamese).

191 "The Whole World Was Watching" by Lance Morrow, *Time,* August 26, 1996. © 1996 Time Inc. Reprinted by permission.

198 From *Born on the Fourth of July* by Ron Kovic. Reprinted by permission of The McGraw-Hill Companies.

206 "The Ballad of the Green Berets" by Barry Sadler and Robin Moore. Courtesy of Eastaboga Music.

207 "I-Feel-Like-I'mFixin'-to-Die Rang" words/music by Joe McDonald. © 1965, renewed 1993 Alkatraz Korner Music BMI. Reprinted by permission.

208 "Fortunate Son" by John C. Fogerty. © 1969 Jondora Music, renewed 1997. Used by permission. All rights reserved.

218 "Not a Dove, But No Longer a Hawk" by Neil Sheehan, *The New York Times,* October 9, 1966. Copyright © 1966 by The New York Times Co. Reprinted by permission.

228 From *America's Longest War,* 2E by George C. Herring. Reprinted by permission of The McGraw-Hill Companies.

237 From "We Are Mired in Stalemate...": "Who, What, When, Where, Why" by Walter Cronkite, (CBS Broadcast, February 27, 1968), *The New York Times and CBS News, The War in Vietnam: A Multi-Media Chronicle.* CBS News & New York Times (Macmillan Digital USA CD-ROM 1995).

240 "Ex-GI Tells of Killing Civilians at Pinkville" by Seymour M. Hersh, *St. Louis Post-Dispatch,* November 25, 1969. Reprinted with permission of the St. Louis Post-Dispatch, copyright 1969.

247 From *Bloods* by Wallace Terry. Copyright © 1984 by Wallace Terry. Reprinted by permission of Random House, Inc.

254 "Vietnam Peace Pacts Signed: America's Longest War Halts" by Flora Lewis, *The New York Times,* January 28, 1973. Copyright © 1973 by The New York Times Co. Reprinted by permission.

260 From *Our Great Spring Victory: An Account of the Liberation of South Vietnam* by General Van Tien Dung, translated by John Spragens, Jr. Copyright © 1999 by Monthly Review. Reprinted by permission of Monthly Review Foundation and Cora Weiss.

270 From *In Country* by Bobbie Ann Mason. Copyright © 1985 by Bobbie Ann Mason.

280 "Can Vietnam Forget?" by Kevin Whitelaw. Copyright, August 10, 1998, *U.S. News & World Report.* Visit us at our Web site at www.usnews.com for additional information. Reprinted by permission.

Photo Research Diane Hamilton

Photos Courtesy of the Library of Congress and the National Archives.

Every effort has been made to secure complete rights and permissions for each selection presented herein. Updated acknowledgements, if needed, will appear in subsequent printings.

Index